# PIMPED

THE SHOCKING TRUE STORY OF THE GIRL
SOLD FOR SEX BY HER BEST FRIEND

# PIMPED

## Samantha Owens

### with Rikki Loftus

JOHN BLAKE

Published by John Blake Publishing,
2.25, The Plaza,
535 Kings Road,
Chelsea Harbour,
London, SW10 0SZ

www.johnblakebooks.com

www.facebook.com/johnblakebooks 
twitter.com/jblakebooks 

First published in paperback in 2019

PB ISBN: 978 1 78946 056 8
Ebook ISBN: 978 1 78946 069 8

British Library Cataloguing-in-Publication Data:
A catalogue record for this book is available from the British Library.

Design by www.envydesign.co.uk

Printed and bound in Great Britain by Clays Ltd, Elcograf S p. A

1 3 5 7 9 10 8 6 4 2

Every attempt has been made to contact relevant copyright-holders, but some were
unobtainable. We would be grateful if the appropriate people could contact us.

John Blake Publishing is an imprint of Bonnier Books UK
www.bonnierbooks.co.uk

To all survivors – thank you for coming forward. Your stories helped me to heal. My only hope is that mine can do the same for you.

# CONTENTS

# PROLOGUE

**W**ith my head down I was led into the bedroom by my wrist, only daring to glance up through my hair once the door was closed. Nervously, I looked around. It seemed like somebody had made a half-hearted attempt to make it look like a real room. A red, patterned rug zigzagged across the floor, but it did little to cover the laminate that was peeling away at the corners. A stale, damp stench filled my nostrils. It smelt like someone had sprayed air freshener to mask it and it lodged in the back of my throat and made me feel sick.

On the far side of the room, a single mattress had been pushed up against a wall. I turned to face the man who had led me there; he was fat and ugly and, as I peered at his lined face, I guessed he was in his thirties, maybe forties. The man pointed at the bare mattress and, reluctantly, I lay down. He pulled down his trousers and I winced as he lay on top of me, his weight crushing my chest, but I didn't dare tell him. How could I? I knew by now there was no use fighting it. My scrawny frame would be no match for the various older men who were skulking around the house.

Instead I lay in silence as he tugged at my knickers and entered me. His stubbly beard was rough and itchy against my face and I noticed he had a hole in one of his bottom teeth. He was disgusting and I shivered as he writhed around on top of me, goosebumps crawling up my arms.

I forced myself to focus on the ceiling and saw a large patch of mould spreading above me. That's what the smell is, I realised, almost grateful for the distraction. The drunken haze I was in helped my mind to drift and I squeezed my eyes shut, willing the nightmare to be over.

Afterwards, he got up and left without a word, leaving me alone in the frozen room. My crotch stung as if it had been punched, and now, finally on my own, I curled myself into a ball. I could hear footsteps outside the bedroom door, laughter echoing around the house. I flinched, praying they wouldn't come in. I was in too much pain. I was just a child and I had no idea where I was, having been directed to the godforsaken place hours earlier. But this night wasn't anything out of the ordinary. This was my norm.

Being sent to houses to be abused by older men was something I had been conditioned to accept and, for a while, I convinced myself I was the one in control. You're not using me, I'm using you, I'd tell myself over and over. I didn't understand that, at the tender age of thirteen, I had been sucked into a child sex ring.

For three years my supposed best friend took me to places around Sheffield to be abused. I was passed from house to house like a toy and, with nowhere else to turn, I came to expect the treatment I received. The youngest of the men were in their twenties and the oldest about sixty. Most of them were Asian, not that it mattered. The one thing they all had in common was the cold look in their eyes as they hurt me.

At my lowest point I believed I'd either be killed or die alone in one of those dilapidated houses. But I survived. By the time the trial of my abusers broke the headlines, I was free from their clutches. For me, the abuse I suffered is in the past but it is still a reality for many young girls in Britain today and that is why I am sharing my story.

For any girl out there who has been through a similar ordeal, I want you to know that I'm with you. Suffering the aftermath of sexual abuse can feel like the loneliest torment in the world, but you are not alone. I want my story to be a reminder that justice can be sought and a victim's voice will be heard. I may be a victim, but I'm also a survivor – and that is something I will carry with me forever.

# 1.

# EARLY DAYS

L ife for me had been chaotic from the start.

I was born in Grimsby, a coastal town in the northeast of England, and I was the first of what would become a brood of six loud and rowdy children. My mum had me when she was just eighteen and, while I never knew my real dad, Mum met Mike in a pub when I was six months old and he became the only dad I've ever known. I was four when we moved to Conway Avenue, and that was the first place I remember calling home. It was a three-bedroom house at the end of a row of terraces. Our nan lived in the house opposite and Auntie Tracey, Mum's sister, was only a few doors away. I loved it.

Grimsby in the nineties was a quiet town and as my siblings, David and Toni, came along in quick succession, we were often left to create our own fun. I was a boisterous child, which made me unpopular with the other girls at school, but that never bothered me because I had David. The pair of us were as thick as thieves and Mum despaired when we'd return home covered in mud and dirt, laughing and play-fighting until one of us got hurt. On the days when David and I fell out, I'd sit alone in my room playing 'My Little Pony'. I dreamed of becoming a vet, rescuing broken animals and nursing them back to health. I pretended the toy ponies were my patients, giving them CPR and imagining I'd saved them.

While Mum stayed home to look after the babies, Dad worked hard to make ends meet. Whether it was in factories or picking up odd jobs, he always brought money home to support us. Mum was always pregnant but, despite her being at home, she wasn't maternal and she always seemed frustrated when we were around.

After school each day we were sent to our rooms to play, but I shared a room with Toni, who was three years younger than me, and I hated her getting into my things. One day I took a marker pen out of my colouring set and drew a black line across the floor to mark our respective sides of the room. I thought it would keep Toni away from my toys, but when Mum found out she hit the roof and we scrubbed to get the ink out of the carpet.

In the evenings I sat in my room hoping Dad wasn't working late so I'd have someone to tuck me into bed, but the days were often spent running around playing tig with David and the kids on the street.

# EARLY DAYS

'Don't go past the green box!' Mum would shout from the living room as we'd dart out the front door. The big electrical box on the corner of the street marked the end of our territory and staying within the boundary created a stretch of road we were free to play in. It felt like a safe haven. Nan would wave to us from her window and, in the summer holidays, Grandad would come out with ice cream for all the local kids. It was great.

I was friends with a girl called Emily, who lived down the road. She was three years older than me but had learning difficulties and that meant she often found herself on her own. I felt sorry for her and I always made sure to say yes when she wanted me to come over. It was a time of pure innocence, laughing and playing with Emily, but that came to an abrupt end when I was five years old. On a day like any other, I went round for a playdate at her house after school. As I sat cross-legged in my red jumper and grey skirt on her bedroom floor, she pulled down the toys from her shelves before turning her attention back to me.

'Do you want me to show you something?' she asked, sitting herself down beside me. I nodded. What happened next is a blur. It's as though my memory was completely wiped, but the next thing I remember I was running home. Mum and Dad were both on the sofa, brew in hand, chatting to my nan who was sat in the armchair, when I came scurrying through the door.

'Mum!' I shouted as I rushed into the living room. 'Mum! Emily did something today.'

'What did she do, Sammy?' Mum asked, not paying much attention. I could tell I was interrupting their conversation. Toni was two years old and was curled up next to Dad.

'She put her fingers in my mini-moo,' I replied, pointing at my school skirt. I immediately had everyone's attention.

'What do you mean?' she asked, glancing at my dad, who stared back at her in silence. 'Don't be telling me porkie pies.'

'I'm not telling porkies,' I protested. 'She put them inside.' I didn't understand why they didn't believe me but Mum marched me to my room and ordered me to stay there until I 'told the truth'. Confused, I threw myself onto my bed. Have I done something wrong? I thought to myself. I wished I hadn't told them. By now, my crotch was hurting and, in pain, I curled myself into a ball.

But I wasn't on my own for long, as I heard the bedroom door creak open and David's happy face appeared from the other side. I smiled.

'What's wrong?' he asked, joining me on my *Teletubbies* duvet.

'Mum says I'm telling porkies but I'm not.' I sighed.

'About what?' he asked, and I looked at him. David was a year younger than me but sometimes it felt like we were twins. The pair of us were always getting up to mischief, telling Mum fibs to cover for each other, but this was something serious. I knew I could tell David anything, so I did.

'What?' David asked after I told him. He looked at me, confused.

'And it hurts,' I added. Instantly, David sprang to life, racing out of the room.

'No!' I begged, chasing after him, but before I could grab him he had fled downstairs. I stood at the top of the stairs, hugging the banister as I listened.

'Mum,' David announced, opening the living room door, 'Sammy's hurt.' Amidst the arguing that followed between my parents, I heard my nan take charge of the situation.

'You need to get her to a doctor,' she told my mum.

The next day, Mum took me to see the GP. I wriggled uncomfortably on the table as the doctor examined me. I felt embarrassed, like it was my fault we were all there.

'Her hymen is broken,' she confirmed, and my mum's face dropped. I didn't know what that meant but Mum took me home where she ran me a bath to soothe the pain. For a few days after that, the adults would talk about me with the door closed, although I didn't quite understand why. I was banned from seeing Emily and, soon after, we moved to a house nearby, in Morpeth Walk.

After the incident, Mum began to take me to the doctor's a lot.

'I'll buy you a bag of chips if you're right naughty in this appointment, Sammy,' she promised me.

'Will I get in trouble? I asked, but Mum shook her head. 'I'll only do it as long as I don't get in trouble.'

'No, Sammy, I'll be so proud of you,' she replied. That was all the encouragement I needed, throwing tantrum after tantrum in the doctor's office. I would run around the room, swearing and screaming at my mum while she despaired to the doctor about how unruly I was. One time I even peed; Mum gave me a quid that day. After a few visits, doctors diagnosed me with ADHD. They prescribed Ritalin and Mum was given extra benefit money for it.

Our new house on Morpeth Walk was meant to be a clean slate for us and, at first, Mum took pride in the place. It was another terraced house and Mum decorated the downstairs in chocolate and cream colours with dado rails – which were all the rage back then – running along the walls. She ordered expensive curtains for the living room and, once they were up, the house looked homely. I was given the box room to have as my very own room and, while Mum didn't decorate it, I loved having a space to call my own. We always had dogs and cats running around and I'd sometimes sneak them into my bed to snuggle.

I joined Littlecoates Primary School and, trying on my new blue uniform, I was excited at the prospect of making friends. But at home Mum and Dad were arguing a lot. They'd just had Jordane and a hectic life with four children was starting to take its toll. Dad spent most nights sleeping on his friend Al's settee. I hated it when Dad left, as I had no one to back me up during rows with Mum. During the times when he was gone, Mum would have visits from men who we were made to call 'Uncle', but they rarely stayed more than a couple of weeks before Dad would get wind of what was happening and scare them off.

Dad started to worry that he wouldn't be allowed to see

me if he and Mum split up. At the time it didn't make sense but he would leave me secret notes with his mobile number on them.

'Repeat it to me, Sammy,' he said, and I chanted the number back to him. 'If Mum stops me from seeing you, just give me a ring, okay?'

'I will,' I promised, and he gave my hair a ruffle.

Meanwhile, my new school was hell. I'd so hoped Littlecoates would be a fresh start for me but my nerves had got the better of me and, after wetting myself in the first week, I was everyone's easy target.

'Hey, Outcast Owens,' one of the boys called out to me as I walked through the halls. I ignored it as I pushed past him, deliberately knocking his shoulder as I went.

'Don't touch me, you weirdo,' he shouted, and his friends laughed. I gave him my toughest glare but inside I wanted to cry. In class I had pencil shavings chucked at me, and once, while I sat colouring in, someone even cut my hair. It may seem like small stuff compared to more violent bullying but these incidents destroyed me and reaffirmed that no one liked me.

Meanwhile, Mum had less control over us by the day and, once Brandon was born, there were five of us to chase after and the house was complete chaos. If she shouted at one of us, we'd club together to stick up for each other. David and I were still like two peas in a pod and Mum hated it when we'd gang up against her.

Mum and Dad rowed every day and, one day when I was

nine, I crouched outside their bedroom door, eavesdropping on them as they yelled at each other.

'Right,' I heard my mum say, exasperated. 'That's it, I'm telling her.'

'You're sick,' Dad retorted. 'Why would you tell her?'

Tell who what? I wondered, but half an hour later we were all called to the living room and everything became horrifically clear. Dad refused to come down and, while us four older kids sat squished side by side on the sofa, Mum looked directly at me.

'I'm just going to come out with it,' she said, her voice a monotone. 'Mike's not your dad, Sam.'

'What?' I asked. 'Dad's not my dad?' It was confusing to even say it out loud.

'No, Sam,' Mum replied with no emotion. 'He's everyone else's dad, but he's not yours.' In an instant, my world crumbled around me. It felt like everything I knew to be true was a lie. I knew I had a different last name. I was an Owens, like my mum, while everyone else was named after my dad, but that had always been the norm, so I'd never questioned it. Suddenly it made sense.

'I hate you!' I shouted at her and, distraught, ran to my room. That night, Dad cuddled me for hours.

'Just because I'm not your real father doesn't mean I'm not your dad, Sammy,' he calmly reassured me. 'I'm always going to be your dad. Nothing's going to change.' I desperately wanted to believe him but it wasn't true. After Mum's revelation, everything changed.

# EARLY DAYS

Not only was I 'Outcast Owens' at school, I became an outcast at home too. David and I had never been so distant – the pair of us used to be inseparable but now he didn't want anything to do with me. While the bullies terrorised me at school, David had made lots of new friends. Previously we'd play together at break time but now he was off playing football on the school field with his new mates, so I spent most days sitting in the toilets on my own. For the first time, I found myself completely alone and I thought no one in the world cared.

Left to entertain myself, I started looking for new places to hide and discovered a secluded spot behind the school where the teachers went to smoke. The next day, I brought one of Dad's lighters along. I picked up a fag end from the floor and lit it. I'd watched Mum and Dad smoke countless times; it looked easy. I put the cigarette to my lips, inhaled and spluttered out a cough. That's gross, I thought. It was like ash burning in my mouth but I liked feeling grown up. On my way home from school, I collected as many fag ends as I could find on the ground, and every day I went back to my secret hideout to smoke them.

My small act of rebellion was a way for me to take back some control. I went to school to be terrorised by kids and then came home to have an argument with David and Toni. I didn't have an escape. Most nights, when I got home, I'd run upstairs to hide in my room, but I think Mum liked that because it kept me quiet in the house.

One evening, I was sitting in my room after school when, all of a sudden, I heard an almighty crash downstairs followed by screams. The four of us older kids simultaneously sprinted from our rooms to find out what the commotion was and, as I stepped into the living room, I gasped. Mum was lying on the floor cradling a distressed but unharmed Brandon as he cried. Glass was strewn everywhere as the exposed bay window blew a gale through the house. Someone had hurled a brick into our front room, narrowly missing Brandon while he slept in his Moses basket by the windowsill.

It was an unsettlingly close call. Just a slightly different angle and that brick could have destroyed our family. Mum reported the crime but we never found out who did it. I felt sick knowing they were still out there – they knew where we lived and they could attack us whenever they wanted. We weren't a liked family in the area; Mum had a reputation for sleeping around and I was targeted by bullies every day – it could have been anyone.

Watching Mum cradle Brandon for dear life was the most maternal I'd ever seen her, and probably ever would see her. The window was boarded up and everything else started to deteriorate. While we still had nice things, Mum gave up on taking care of the place. With us kids running around, she just couldn't keep on top of it and soon the house was filthy. The floor was a sea of unwashed clothes and dog poo and we couldn't move around for fear of stepping on something unpleasant. It was disgusting. The babies would crawl around in wee and poo but Mum didn't care. Even if I did have any friends to bring round, I would be too embarrassed to do so. On the rare occasion when I'd find a clean top that had been dumped on the floor, I'd lift it up and realise, oh no, it's got dog shit on it. The walls were stained with filth and it wasn't long before the rats and mice got in.

The only solace I had was my secret cigarettes. I'd watched my mum roll a fag before, knocking the crumbs into her baccy tray, and when she wasn't looking I started using the leftovers to roll my own. I'd sneak into the kitchen for a smoke once a day. I don't know how I was never caught but Mum and Dad were usually too busy at each other's throats to notice. I was nine years old when one day I spotted some green stuff in the tray. I didn't know what it was but I knew Mum used it, so I added it to my rollie and took a drag. Suddenly the room started to spin and I giggled. In my dizzy high, everything that was weighing me down, the bullies, the arguing, seemed to slip away and nothing else mattered. From that day on, weed was my new escape, and every chance I got to steal it from Mum and Dad, I did.

When Mum and Dad fell out, a new man would arrive to take Dad's place and there was always something strange about the guys Mum brought into the house. I was nine when the first one moved in, and I couldn't believe what I was seeing when he walked about the house naked. We saw everything. He'd potter about in the kitchen completely in the buff, exposing his fat, round belly with his bits poking out underneath. He was disgusting. Us kids avoided him at all costs, but when he did catch us sitting on the sofa or watching TV, he'd place himself down beside us, completely naked, and start cutting into his thighs. He was a self-harmer, slicing his arms and legs in front of us until we screamed.

'Mum, he's doing it again!' I'd shout, legging it away from him as soon as he started cutting. She'd move him away but ultimately did nothing to stop it. It was as if she didn't care. I rang Dad on the landline to tell him what was happening and he came round like a shot to chase him out. Dad moved back in for a while but it wasn't long before he was back on Al's sofa again.

Once he was gone another man moved in and Mum insisted we called him 'Dad'. It was confusing but, by then, Chelsea had been born and Mum pretended to us that the new guy was Chelsea's real dad. With his long greasy hair and big brown boots, we nicknamed him 'Cowboy', but behind his back we referred to him as 'the freakazoid'. He was just as weird as the self-harmer, strutting around the house in shorts so tiny we could see his willy. David, Toni and I would snigger at him as he sat down, exposing himself. It was vile. Mum allowed Cowboy to bath us, and every night I would throw a tantrum in protest. I didn't want him to touch me. The relationship didn't last long because as soon as Dad found out he kicked off and Cowboy ran for the hills. After that, Dad moved home yet again but still he and Mum couldn't find a way to sort out their differences. When I was ten years old, Dad sat me down and handed me a mobile phone.

'Sammy, this has to be our secret,' he told me. 'If Mum finds this she'll take it off you but you need it to get in touch with me.' I slowly took the phone from him.

'Does this mean you're leaving?' I asked, and Dad nodded.

'I am,' he sighed, before pointing towards the phone. 'But that's why I got you this.'

'So, I can ring you whenever?' I asked tentatively, and Dad smiled, wiping the tears from my eyes. I had memorised his number long before this day.

'Of course,' he replied, giving me a cuddle. 'Everything will be alright and, if it's not, ring me.'

It was the worst day of my life, waving goodbye to my lovely dad. The only sense of stable love I got was from him and now he was leaving. I begged Mum to make him stay but I knew it was too late – he'd had enough. Watching him go, I felt sick, like my only protector was walking out the door.

## 2.

# SHEFFIELD

With Dad gone, Mum didn't have anyone to help rein us in, so us six kids ran riot around the house. By this point, she had mentally checked out, sometimes even forgetting to pick the younger ones up from school. She'd started having trouble with social services and we were all labelled 'at risk', so I would wag school to make sure she didn't fall asleep or forget to pick the other kids up again. Not that I'd wanted to go to school anyway. Littlecoates Primary had become my living nightmare but sometimes Mum would bribe me with sweets and money to go in although, after some time, even that didn't work anymore.

'What will it take for you to go to school, Sam?' Mum asked me. She knew social services wouldn't be happy if I played truant.

'Buy me twenty fags and I'll go in,' I replied bluntly.

# PIMPED

At first she was shocked, but she'd long since given up on caring. If it meant getting me out of the house and getting social services off her back, she'd do it, and eventually she started buying me packs of cigarettes.

Even then I didn't always go to my lessons; instead I'd sneak round to my spot behind the school and smoke. If another kid ever saw me, I'd just scowl at them until they fled. No one ever told the teachers what I was doing but, even if they knew, they never did anything about it. I was small and scrawny but I tried my best to look hard. I much preferred it for the kids at school to fear me rather than bully me.

At home, Mum had stopped cooking us our tea after school, leaving it to me to pick up the slack. I was only ten years old and didn't know what I was doing so, more often than not, the six of us lived on toast and cereal. Every now and then I'd try my best to make a proper meal but the cooking oil would spit at me and hurt my face. The times when Mum did cook, she only ever made egg and chips, and we always complained that she didn't do the yolk right.

Mum had more men than ever coming round to the house, and she wasn't shy about having sex in front of us. This had become the norm, and we thought nothing of watching cartoons in the living room as Mum romped with a stranger in the corner. David and I bonded over our mutual hatred for Mum's many boyfriends and soon the pair of us were back to our old selves.

'I've just spat in his cereal, what shall we do next?' David quizzed, a wicked glint in his eye.

'Let's put toothpaste in his shoe,' I suggested, and we both giggled. Having David back was like having my right arm reattached, and he was the only one who would stick up for me against Mum. Back together, the two of us were worse than ever and we were hell-bent on bullying Mum's boyfriends.

One day, we heard her latest bloke start to run a bath before heading into Mum's bedroom. Seizing our chance, David sprinted to the bathroom and peed in the tub. Afterwards we sat crouched behind my bedroom door, our hands cupped to our mouths, smothering the giggles. Hearing him walk back into the bathroom, we held our breath, preparing for the worst, but the next thing we heard was the sound of water splashing as he plonked himself down in the tub. David and I stared at each other in silent screams of laughter. When he finally got out, we listened from my door as he spoke to our mum on the landing.

'I tell you what, love,' we heard him say. 'I feel so much better now, nice and clean.' Unable to suppress it any longer, we both burst into roaring fits of laughter, howling at the thought of him bathing in David's wee.

'Daft kids,' our mum remarked, but that only made us cackle harder. I clutched my sides, in stitches from laughing so much. Having David back was ace.

We were determined to make sure Mum's bloke left as soon as possible but, once one was gone, he would swiftly be replaced by another. A strategy David and I discovered as one sure way to wind them up was to throw their belongings into the big bush in the back garden. They'd spend hours and even days tearing their hair out and starting rows with Mum to find their shoes, wallets or clothes. One guy constantly listened to Conway Twitty's American country music and it drove us mad until we snapped his CD and threw it into the bush.

'This is our house,' I told David defiantly, marvelling at all the things we'd hidden from Mum's boyfriends. 'And I want them to know it.'

I was eleven when Mum moved Joe in. At seventeen years old, he was just six years my senior and twelve years my mum's junior but he immediately started acting as if he were our dad. Joe was short and quite fat, and would stomp about the place demanding we listen to him.

'You're not my dad,' I'd argue back when he tried to get me to tidy my room.

'If I'm not your dad, then where is he?' Joe callously replied. 'He's not here, so you answer to me.'

Despite how much Joe seemed to despise David and me, he was perfect with the younger kids. Once again, Mum told us he was Chelsea's real dad and we were still at an age where we blindly believed everything she said. Chelsea was quite a poorly baby, born tiny and premature, and the rest of us were always extra careful around her, so we decided to make the best of our situation with Joe.

For a while, life wasn't too bad. Whenever I got fed up with Mum and Joe, I'd message Dad on my secret phone and he'd let me go round to his house. He was staying just four streets away, and when I'd go over for a visit he'd preach to me about life.

'Nothing is free in this world, Sammy, so be careful,' he'd tell me, and I'd roll my eyes.

'Yeah, Dad, I know.' I'd heard this lecture a thousand times, although listening to Dad's rants was always better than being bossed around by Joe.

Come summer, I was due to go on a camping trip with my school year group and, for once, I was excited about something to do with school. The idea of no parents telling me what to do, and no kids to look after, seemed like heaven and I started packing weeks beforehand, carefully considering what to take. Meticulously picking out my favourite clothes, I looked around my plain room. There was no indication that I lived there; it just looked like any other box room.

'Come on, Sam,' Mum announced, marching into my room on the day of the trip. 'Let's get you ready to go.' She bundled all of my clothes into bin bags, tying them up as she went.

'Do I need to take everything?' I asked, put out by the work I'd already put in to organising what I was taking.

'Yes,' Mum confirmed. 'Just in case.' I didn't argue with her; if taking everything with me meant I got to escape for a few days, then it was worth it. Lugging my clothes down the stairs, I was greeted with even more black bags and it looked as though the whole house had been packed up.

'Right, kids,' Mum ordered, 'everyone take what you can carry.' To me she added, 'Are you excited?' I grinned, nodding back at her. 'Good, let's go.'

Clutching my bags, we headed to Grimsby Town station. Everyone was lugging about three bin bags each, heaving them into the train carriage. I don't know how it didn't click, but I was still young and naive enough to believe that Mum would never lie to me.

'I can't wait to go on my trip,' I declared to David. The excitement of travelling on the train was making me even more eager.

'Where are you going on this trip?' David asked, and I realised that I didn't know. I shrugged.

'I'll find out when I get there.' I smiled at him and turned to peer out of the window. Anywhere away from here will be good, I thought to myself.

Ninety minutes later, we arrived in Sheffield and, dragging our luggage off the train, we followed Mum out of the station and through the streets until we reached a grey building.

We waited around while Mum spoke to some grown-ups, and, eventually, we found ourselves in a small flat.

'Okay,' Mum stated, after we'd heaved our things into the living room. 'You all need to help me unpack the bags.'

'Erm, aren't you taking me on my trip?' I asked, confused as to what we were doing in this new place. I'd started to worry I was going to miss it. Mum was already in the middle of emptying a black bag when she turned to me, nonchalantly.

'Sam, I'm sorry,' she said, and my heart started to sink. 'There is no school trip. This is where we live now.' Overwhelmed with disappointment, I felt tears prick my eyes, but that quickly turned into anger.

'You bitch,' I shouted at her and, before I could stop myself, I slapped her across the face. For a few seconds both Mum and I stood shocked at what I'd done before I fled into another room, not wanting to cry in front of her.

After that, life was set on a downward spiral. Where we now lived was in council housing, a block of flats in Netherthorpe that was a far cry from our home in Morpeth Walk, when Dad was still around. It was dingy, with three bedrooms, which meant I no longer had my own room. Joe arrived a few days after we moved in and he and Mum took the master bedroom. David and Brandon shared another, leaving the third bedroom to Toni, Jordane, Chelsea and me. It was cramped to say the least. There were two bunk beds, with me on the bottom below Jordane. I hated it.

Compared to Grimsby, Sheffield was a big city, and in the late nineties and early noughties it had a high rate of immigration, predominantly Pakistani. Grimsby was a sleepy town and, before moving, I had never even noticed anyone of a different race in the neighbourhood. But when I started my new school at Firth Park Academy, I was the only white person there. There had been a small-minded mentality in Grimsby about immigration but it didn't bother me – although, by then, it was rare if I attended school at all. Instead, David and I would catch the bus into town and smoke together.

# PIMPED

The Peace Gardens was a stretch of grass in Sheffield city centre that became our favourite place to spend the day, running wild on our own and hiding from the police, who would take us home. Getting caught by the cops one too many times playing truant, I was seen as a problem child but, because I was also labelled 'at risk', social workers started to take an interest in me and I began having regular contact with them.

Meanwhile, Joe had started going on burglaries late at night, and by the time I was eleven he was taking David and me along with him. On foot, he'd lead us to abandoned buildings where we'd break in, wandering around aimlessly and robbing whatever we could sell. I enjoyed the sense of belonging I got from Joe taking us out with him, and for the first time I felt I was being treated like a grown-up. Mum and I didn't get on at all by now and one night, after a routine argument with her, I stormed off with Joe to his dad's house. I knew his sister, Sabrina, and the pair of us were sat laughing in her bedroom when Joe appeared with a bottle of vodka.

'Shall we get this party started?' Joe chuckled, passing the bottle to Sabrina.

'Here,' Sabrina gestured the bottle towards me, after taking a glug, 'have a swig.' Usually it would be my mum drinking with them instead of me, so I was delighted to be included. I was only eleven and, while I smoked, I had never tried alcohol. I put the bottle to my lips and took a sip. The vodka burned my throat. That's disgusting, I thought to myself. My face gave away my thoughts and both Sabrina and Joe laughed. The taste was foul but I felt cool drinking it, so I continued until the three of us had finished the bottle.

Barely able to stand, I excused myself to go to the toilet, but no sooner was I through the bathroom door than I noticed Joe had followed me in. Surprised, I turned to look at him and, without warning, he grabbed my face and kissed me. I was stunned and, unsure of what was happening, I froze and he kissed me again. He had never given me any indication before that night that he fancied me and it felt weird. He's my mum's boyfriend, I thought, as he kissed me for the third time before moving away.

'Don't tell anyone,' he instructed. Giving me a wink, he left the bathroom and I listened as his footsteps drifted downstairs. I couldn't tell if I felt sick about the situation or if that was the vodka, so I wandered back into Sabrina's bedroom. She peered up at me from where she was lying on the floor.

'Sabrina, your brother just kissed me,' I announced. I wanted to gauge her reaction; if she was angry then I'd know it was wrong.

'Oh my God, did he?' she replied, with excitement in her voice. 'Cute.'

After that, I didn't tell anyone what Joe had done. I was at an age where everyone at school had started to get boyfriends and I naively hoped that Joe could be mine. Over the next few weeks, Joe's burglaries became an excuse to get me on my own, kissing me the minute David wasn't there. I still wasn't sure how I felt about it but I convinced myself we were dating, and the fact that we had to keep it a secret made it seem romantic.

Growing up, I'd watched relationships play out on TV and I loved the idea of having someone I loved to cuddle up with at the end of the day, and that's what I thought Joe would be. I imagined us walking hand in hand through town, going for posh meals or cinema dates. It was never like that but he called me his little princess, and after every time we snogged he'd buy me a new pair of trainers or some make-up. It was the only relationship I'd ever known and, in my childish fantasy, I thought that meant we were in love. He sent me text messages saying he loved me and he even started cornering me at home. Joe was obsessed with the singer Tiffany and whenever he'd catch me on my own in the house, he'd whisper her lyrics to me.

'I think we're alone now,' he hissed, following me into the kitchen. 'There doesn't seem to be anyone around.' I squirmed uncomfortably as Joe forced his arms around my waist, his hands wandering over me.

'Mum might come in, though,' I protested, wriggling free from his grasp. I was so confused by Joe. The way he treated me felt weird but, amidst the rowing I did with Mum and looking after the other kids, I started to enjoy the attention I got from him. It felt like someone was finally appreciating me.

# SHEFFIELD

Social services had been visiting a lot and they weren't happy with the environment in which Mum was raising us. In one of our meetings, I made a point of lighting up a fag in front of them and smoking it. They won't like this, I thought, looking the social worker in the eye as I took a long drag of the cigarette. I glanced over at Mum on the other side of the table, and she didn't bat an eyelid. After that, it wasn't long before social services started taking an extra interest in me and, within weeks, one of the social workers offered to take me for a day out. With the promise of Maccy D's, I couldn't refuse.

'I thought we'd pay my friend Pat a visit first,' she told me once we were in the car.

I shrugged. 'Sure,' I replied, smiling to myself. I was excited at the thought of getting away for the day. Anywhere that didn't involve Mum sounded good to me.

As soon as we arrived at Pat's house, she swung open the door and greeted me with a warm hug. She was an older Asian woman with silver streaks running through her long black hair. Her fingers were covered in rings and she wore bracelets that jingled as she walked. Wow, I thought to myself. She's so nice. Pat invited me into the living room, where she brought me a cup of tea.

'I'll just go pick us up the McDonald's, then,' the social worker said, excusing herself from the house. McDonald's was only over the road but she didn't come back for two hours. In that time, Pat and I chatted about all sorts. She was interested in what I liked to do, and when I told her all about mine and David's antics, she thought it was funny. I beamed, completely at ease. After we'd eaten, Pat left the room and my social worker turned to look at me.

'So,' she started, giving me a grin. 'Do you think you'd like to live with Pat?' The question caught me off guard but I instantly envisioned what life would be like with her. There would be no more cooking or taking care of the other kids; there wouldn't be any more rows with my mum and, of course, I'd be away from Joe. I loved my siblings dearly but I wasn't even a teenager yet and I wanted the freedom to be a kid myself again.

'Yes,' I finally responded after mulling it over. 'I'd really love to live with Pat.'

'That's fantastic,' she replied, calling Pat back into the room, who gave me a tight squeeze.

'Welcome home,' Pat cooed. She showed me to my new bedroom and I couldn't believe it. I had my own TV, my own wardrobe. There'd be no little kids running about because I had a lock on my door. Looking around, I gaped in awe. Is this really mine? I thought in disbelief, but it was. It was my very own room and that was the best feeling in the world. It was paradise, like I had really finally found my home.

# 3.

# LIFE IN CARE

L ife at Pat's was a world away from living with Mum. There were rules and schedules we were expected to follow and, for once, my life had structure. Pat made us dinner every night and we always had the choice between two meals. There were always at least two other foster kids living in the house and, even though the other kids never stayed for long, Pat made it feel like a family.

'Dinner's ready!' she'd shout, her sing-song voice chirping around the house. Pat made amazing corned beef hash and, sitting down to eat, it truly felt like a proper home. Pat's house was the most stable place I had ever lived, and for the first six months I didn't even see my siblings. It didn't bother me too much. I missed them but I didn't miss the screaming, shouting and nappy changing, and I knew full well that's exactly what I'd be expected to do if I went to visit, so I didn't. Besides, I was far too in love with my new life with Pat to worry about what was happening at home. I hardly thought of Mum at all.

Even though I had a new sense of stability, Pat still couldn't tell me what to do.

'I'm going out,' I'd announce, running down the stairs to put my shoes on at the front door.

'Okay, Sam,' Pat would call out from the living room. She would always remind me, 'Just please make sure you come back before curfew.'

Pat tried to impose a curfew of 8 p.m. but it was rare that I ever made it back in time. She wasn't able to actually enforce it, and I came and went as I pleased. My attendance at school was the lowest it had ever been and, as I headed out the door one time, Pat called after me.

'Are you going to school tomorrow?' she asked.

'Not likely,' I muttered. I'd completely lost interest in school.

'Come on,' Pat persisted, following me outdoors. 'You'll regret not going to school, Sam. What about your future?'

I could tell she only had my best interests at heart but nothing in the world could make me go to school. Not batting so much as an eyelid, I shrugged at her indifferently.

'I'll just become a drug dealer or a gangster,' I replied, tongue in cheek. I knew it was stupid but I didn't care. I just wanted to be left alone. Pat tutted at me but didn't pester me any further about school. I guess it worked, as I played truant almost every day.

# LIFE IN CARE

My stay at Pat's was a temporary solution and, after a few months, I was moved to a new children's home in Shiregreen. The woman who ran the home was also called Pat, but she was nothing like the caring and motherly Pat I'd grown to love. Instead, she was snappy and bossy, so I nicknamed her 'Nasty Pat'.

I hated Nasty Pat and, at the age of thirteen, I started getting the bus back to Mum's to escape. Handing the bus driver 40p, I'd make the journey home but, just like I'd expected, my visits were spent chasing after the kids, constantly trying to do everything my mum was neglecting. By now, Brandon was five and Chelsea was three, and the pair of them were screaming at the top of their lungs, getting louder and louder the longer they were left unattended.

'Will you both just shut up?' I snapped, but instantly felt guilty for shouting; they got enough of that from Mum but I didn't know how else to discipline them. Even after moving out, I was still a child bringing up Mum's children. Sneaking a glance on the kitchen counter, I noticed a pack of fags next to Mum's baccy tray, where a stash of her weed also lay. Bingo. Swiping the goods, I scarpered, afraid I'd go insane if I stayed any longer.

Even though I hated being at Mum's house, seeing the state of filth the kids were left in pricked my conscience and I began popping over quite regularly. It wasn't long, however, before all the kids were taken into care. Mum ranted about an anonymous tip-off that had been made to social services.

'When I find out who it is,' she raved down the phone, 'there'll be hell to pay.'

Social services had lots of files on Mum from over the years, and as more children had been added to the brood the catalogue of neglect had built up. There were incidents of Brandon wandering the streets in nothing but a soiled nappy. As a baby, Chelsea had been spotted on a visit screaming naked in her pram, no nappy on and with sunburn across her chest. Recently when they'd set foot in Mum's festering flat, it was a no brainer – something had to change and, because of the living conditions, all six of us were placed in care.

I relaxed a little, knowing the kids were now being cared for. We were taken to contact centres once or twice a week to see each other and I spent all week looking forward to those visits. Chelsea, Brandon, Jordane and Toni were kept together while David and I were placed in separate homes. We were the only ones separated because we were so terrible together, so I treasured the moments when everyone was reunited for an hour or so a week. Even without our parents we were close knit, and when the six of us were all together we were a family again.

Now that I was back in touch with David, we started going into town together a lot. He lived in a children's home in Stocksbridge, on the outskirts of Sheffield, so we met at the Peace Gardens in the city centre and spent the day wreaking havoc. With nothing else to do, we wandered into shops, egging each other on to nick sweets or cans of Coke. We never got away with it. Instead, we laughed as we were chased out of the stores, dropping our stolen things as we went. As care kids, if we didn't go home at night, we were reported missing and, if found, we'd be sent back to our foster homes. So when a police officer spotted David walking around in town, he snatched him before he could get away.

'Come on, then,' the officer said to David, giving him a small smile. 'We've got to take you home.' That day, there was a group of us messing about and we cheered as the police guided David away.

'Yeah, look at me,' David shouted, loving the attention. 'I'm getting arrested.' We laughed. He wasn't actually getting arrested but, to us, getting taken away by the police was bragging rights and we all thought David looked cool being escorted home.

By now, aged thirteen, I had discovered make-up and was starting to get a lot of male attention. Some of the guys who hung around me and David would compliment me on my looks and tell me how pretty I was. It was embarrassing to hear but, at the same time, it was flattering, as I longed to be popular. One day, David and I were walking from the Peace Gardens to the shops when we spotted a girl smoking by the entrance to the indoor markets. She was sat on top of a bin, wearing tight jeans and a crop top, with massive hoops hanging from her ears. Her black hair was tied into a ponytail on the side of her head and she was surrounded by a group of men. She looked so popular and, instantly, I wished I was her.

'I dare you to go over and get a fag.' David nudged me, pointing towards the girl. I burst out laughing.

'No way! I dare you to go and get a fag,' I retorted. Seeing how confident she was, and all of the attention she was getting, I was intimidated. There was no chance that I'd dare approach her. David was only twelve but he wasn't fazed by her.

'Fine, I'll do it,' he replied and, with that, he sauntered over to her with his cocky attitude. 'Yo baby, have you got a fag?' he asked, nonchalantly leaning against one of the market stalls. The girl chuckled and reached over to pass him a cigarette. I wandered over next to David and she turned to look at me.

'Why aren't you at school?' she asked. 'You look a bit young to be hanging around here.' She looked cool but by the way she spoke to us I thought she also might be a bitch.

'We don't go to school,' I responded, trying my best to look aloof.

'Is that right?' she replied, hopping down from the bin to stand next to me. 'I'm Amanda.' David and I introduced ourselves and she smiled at us. 'Okay, David and Samantha, do you want to come shoplifting?' David and I were rubbish at shoplifting but I didn't want to let her down. At fifteen, Amanda was only two years older than me but the way she dressed and acted made her seem so much older and I wanted to impress her.

'Yeah, alright then,' I said, and the three of us headed towards Poundland. Once in the shop, Amanda told us what she wanted us to steal.

'Right, you get that,' she whispered, pointing at a lip gloss, and I shoved it in my pocket while David stuffed his sleeves with other bits of make-up. Amanda left the shop first with the two of us trailing behind. My eyes darted around, scared someone would spot us and, shuffling to the exit, my heart pounded. But once out of the doors, we legged it down the street in fits of laughter. I couldn't believe we'd got away with it.

'We did it!' I exclaimed. I was amazed. David and I had tried it thousands of times but we always got caught.

'Yeah!' Amanda cheered. 'Sick, sick.' We followed her back to the markets, where she showed off to her friends what we'd nabbed.

'Well done, Sammy,' she congratulated, gesturing for me to sit next to her. The markets were held in a large hall and, amongst the hustle and bustle of the meat and dairy vendors, there were a couple of stalls left empty and unoccupied. Having found an abandoned one, Amanda had claimed it for the day as her hangout. To be invited to sit with her felt like I had passed some sort of test and I was ecstatic to be accepted. I took my spot by Amanda's side and she handed me a fag. I stayed there for hours, chatting to her long after David had gone home.

'I've had sex with loads of people,' Amanda bragged to me, pointing out various men around the markets as they passed by. 'I've shagged him . . . and him.'

'Nice one,' I replied, not knowing what to say. I was a virgin, but I sensed Amanda wouldn't think I was cool anymore if she knew that. A group of men started to form around her at one point. They were much older than us, and looked to be at least in their thirties, some even older. I wondered why they wanted to hang around with a couple of kids, but they all fancied Amanda and she seemed to love the attention.

'Nice tits, Amanda,' one guy jeered, grabbing one of her breasts. I was shocked but Amanda wasn't fazed.

'Come here then,' she replied, pushing his head into her cleavage. Everyone fell about laughing and, while I laughed along, I crossed my arms. Not that I had any cleavage yet to grab, but I didn't want anyone trying to touch me. The man lifted his head away from her breasts, mimicking himself gasping for air.

'Suck my dick, Amanda,' he said to her and she nodded, jumping down from the stall.

'Okay, let's go round here.' She gestured outside to an alcove behind the markets before looking back at me. 'I'll be back in a minute, Sammy,' she chimed, and with that she turned on her heels and, grabbing the guy's hand, walked off. I couldn't believe it. *Is she seriously taking him up on that offer?* I was bewildered by how sexual Amanda was. While she was gone, I chatted awkwardly to the other men. I didn't really know what to say, so I was relieved when, ten minutes later, I spotted her heading back towards me.

'He's right big,' she exclaimed, gesturing with her hands. The men sniggered, some shouting about how they felt left out.

'You'll get your turn one day,' she cackled back. Uncomfortable, I laughed along. *If anyone thinks I'll do that, they can piss off.* Breaking my thoughts, Amanda jumped back onto the stall and passed me a small bag of weed.

'Here.' She grinned. 'Will you roll me a joint?' I immediately perked up. Finally something I'm actually good at, I thought, taking out my Rizlas. I rolled the joint and, following Amanda to a secluded spot outside, handed it back to her to light. After a couple of minutes she passed it to me and I took a long drag before handing it along to one of the men. I could feel Amanda watching me as I sat calmly next to her.

'I think there's too much in there,' she said, gesturing to the joint and burying her face in her hands. 'I think I'm whiteying.'

I smirked. After years of smoking my mum's weed I had built up a tolerance but I must have put in more than Amanda was used to.

'Woah!' She marvelled at how laid-back I was. 'You can actually smoke weed.' Afterwards, I listened to her tell everyone how cool I was, and I smiled to myself, secretly thrilled by her approval. By now the markets were closing up for the day and, as the shutters went down on the stalls, we headed back outside. I looked around, realising how dark it was getting. Other groups of men had formed outside the shops. I couldn't see what they were doing but it looked like they were dealing drugs.

'You know what, Sammy,' Amanda said, watching the men as we sat down on the cold concrete, 'I reckon I could sleep with any guy I wanted to.'

'Probably,' I mumbled back. I looked around at the guys she was eyeing up; again, they were all much older than us and I didn't know how she could find them attractive.

'Anyway,' she went on, turning her focus back onto me, 'what was your first time like?' This put me on the spot, and I didn't know what to say.

'It was alright,' I replied, cringing inside. 'It was normal.' I shrugged at her, trying to play it cool, but inside my stomach twisted into anxious knots. I was hoping she didn't see past the lie. Before she could ask me anything further I stopped the conversation in its tracks. 'I should probably go home for my tea now,' I said. I stood up, ready to leave.

'Hang on a sec.' Amanda fished her phone out of her pocket. 'Stick your number in here so I can text you.' I grinned, punching in my phone number before handing the phone back to her.

As I left, I smiled to myself. Amanda was so much cooler and more experienced than me but she wanted to be my friend. Maybe I'll get as popular as her, I mused. Everyone seemed to know her. After watching how confident she was, I decided she was everything I wished I could be. I was excited to have a new friend and, as I headed home, I hoped she'd text me soon.

# 4.

# AMANDA

Desperate to appear cool and experienced in front of Amanda, I enlisted the advice of Briony, another girl at my children's home. She was a few years older than me and I'd spotted her sneaking off at night to visit her boyfriend. I'd seen my mum have sex countless times but I still didn't quite understand it.

'Briony, how do you have sex?' I queried, hovering in her doorway. She was sat on her bed watching TV.

'Basically just do doggy style,' she answered, not bothering to look up from her programme.

'Doggy style? What's doggy style?' I asked, and Briony sighed, glancing over at me.

'Just go on all fours, Sam, the guy will know what to do.'

*Go on all fours?* I wanted to have sex so I could seem more grown up but the idea of actually doing it myself sounded

41

scary. I had thought about what it would be like to lose my virginity, imagining it on a beach somewhere, with candles and roses. It was childish but, at thirteen years old, I held onto that fantasy.

The next morning my phone pinged with a text from Amanda: 'Meet me at the markets at 1?' I beamed. She actually wants to chill with me, I thought to myself, throwing on whatever I could find. I scraped my hair into a side ponytail, just like Amanda's, and headed out of the door. But when I got into town I found her sitting outside the indoor market hall, smoking with another girl.

'This is my friend Olivia,' said Amanda, introducing the girl to me, and I reluctantly smiled at her. Olivia was tall and pretty and, immediately, I was jealous. Why can't I just hang out with Amanda on her own? I thought. I hated the idea of having to compete with Olivia for her attention. Amanda was wearing a tight crop top again and was already getting wolf-whistled by boys walking past. I looked down at my shapeless tracksuit and wished I could look more like her.

'Do you dye your hair, Amanda?' I asked, comparing her jet-black locks with my mousey brown hair.

'Yeah I do,' she replied. 'I can dye yours for you if you want,' she offered. 'So we can be matching.'

'Yeah, go on then,' I coolly accepted, but inside I was ecstatic. Olivia didn't want to dye my hair and I was secretly glad when she left, leaving Amanda and me to rob black hair dye from a shop in town before jumping on the bus to

# AMANDA

Amanda's house. She lived in a children's home in Lowedges and her room was decorated with the Playboy bunny logo.

'Wow,' I marvelled at the girly room. 'Your bedroom is so cool.'

'Thanks,' Amanda said, tearing open the box of hair dye. Her clothes were scattered across the floor and she cleared a corner where we could sit. On the radio, 'Hips Don't Lie' by Shakira blasted out as Amanda got to work, applying the dye to my hair. Once it was washed and dried, I beamed at the sight of my new dark look. Amanda posed beside me in front of the mirror and the pair of us grinned at our reflections.

'See,' she said, putting her head next to mine. 'You can't tell which is my hair and which is yours.'

I smiled. 'We're like twins,' I replied.

Amanda's foster mum had agreed to drop us at the train station so we could head to Meadowhall Shopping Centre and, while Amanda got changed, I went downstairs to wait for her. I had sat myself down at the bottom of the stairs when Amanda's foster mum appeared, beckoning me into the living room.

'Listen, Samantha, I need to talk to you for a second,' she started to say in a lowered voice, as I followed her into the room. Closing the door, she continued: 'I think you should stop hanging around Amanda.'

'What, why?' I asked, baffled by what she was suggesting. 'She's my mate.'

'You don't know her,' her foster mum warned, shaking her head. 'And you don't want to. She's trouble.'

'No she's not,' I protested. I couldn't understand why she wanted me to leave. I'd never had a best friend like Amanda before and I couldn't imagine dropping her.

'I like you, Samantha. I'm not telling you this to be horrible to you.' Then why are you being a bitch? I thought. I didn't respond and, instead, I left her in the living room and went back to sit on the stairs. I couldn't believe it – she was trying to take Amanda away from me. I sat there dwelling on it in anger until Amanda finally came downstairs and her foster mum drove us to the train station.

'Have a good time, girls, stay safe.' She waved good-bye and we headed to Meadowhall. On the way, I felt compelled to tell Amanda what had been said. It would be disloyal not to.

'Fucking hell,' Amanda remarked once she knew. 'What a bitch. She just doesn't want me to have any friends.'

'Yeah, I know.' I nodded my head in agreement. 'Stupid cow.'

After we spent the day shoplifting at the shopping centre, Amanda took me back to the markets to drink and smoke. We hung around outside the market hall with another group of about five men. I didn't recognise this group but they were just as old as the last and, as they passed around bottles of cider, I realised that many of them looked old enough to be our dads. I peered at them, slouching around in tracksuits; they were grubby and unshaven. Why does Amanda flirt with these men? I wondered, repulsed by them all. I couldn't understand what she saw in them but they were offering us alcohol so I sat down beside her, lighting a fag.

Half a bottle into the evening, one of the guys grabbed Amanda out of the blue and pulled down her top. I looked on in shock as he started to suck on her breasts and Amanda burst out laughing. There were still a fair number of shoppers in town and my cheeks burned with second-hand embarrassment in case anyone might catch them. The guy pulled away and, looking around at the other men, I noticed a couple of them were eyeing me up. You better not ask me to do that, I thought, glancing back at Amanda as she adjusted her top. She looked back at me and smirked.

'Oi, Sammy,' she shouted. 'I dare you to kiss him.'

She pointed at an Asian man who had been staring at me. With white hairs dotted about his dark beard, he must have been at least forty. No way, I thought. I'm not doing that. Not moving, I turned to Amanda, hoping she would say it was a joke. But when she stared back at me, her eyebrows raised, I knew that if I didn't do it I would look like a prude. I grimaced, nodding at Amanda.

'Yeah, alright,' I replied, and moved towards the man. He bent down to snog me, forcing his tongue down my throat. His breath was foul but Amanda cheered so, after a few seconds, I broke away from him, grinning at her.

'Easy,' I laughed, sitting back down beside her. I reached for my bottle of cider but Amanda pulled it away.

'No, now you have to go kiss that one,' she said, gesturing to another man. Everything I did with boys was bragging rights but it felt like Amanda was testing my limits. I didn't want to kiss the random men who hung around her but, deep down, I didn't know how to say no. I was so in awe of Amanda that I'd do whatever she asked. Without another thought, I reached over to the middle-aged man she had pointed at and gave him a kiss.

'Yes, Sammy!' Amanda praised me, handing me my cider. 'You did it!'

I chuckled, ignoring the sick feeling in the pit of my stomach, and took a sip of my drink. The conversation quickly turned to Amanda talking about sex again, bragging about all the positions and places she'd had it. I fell quiet but, remembering what Briony had told me at home, I was suddenly eager to join in.

'I always do doggy style,' I chimed in, and Amanda looked impressed with my input.

'Yeah, me too,' she replied, taking a swig from her bottle. 'You're cool, Sammy,' she added. Hearing those words felt like a stamp of approval. 'Do you fancy coming to a party with me?'

'Yeah, of course,' I replied, and my stomach did flips, excited at the thought of going to my first party. 'What will it be like?'

'It'll be right cool,' Amanda explained. 'It's like a club but because we're too young to get in, it's at a house.'

'That sounds ace,' I beamed.

A few nights later, I sat with Amanda in her bedroom, sharing a bottle of vodka. She gave me one of her miniskirts to wear and, once we were drunk enough, she led me to a house on Infirmary Road. I didn't know what to expect but I imagined there would be a lot of people our age, with the girls dressed up just like us, so I was surprised to find there were hardly any girls there at all.

I walked into the smoky house and there must have been about fifty men crammed in, compared to the handful of girls dotted about. All the men there looked Asian and were anywhere from in their thirties to around sixty years old. I'd never been to a party before so I just brushed it off, thinking to myself, I guess there's always more guys than girls at a party.   Feeling confident with Amanda by my side, I strode into the living room where a group of men were sat passing around hashish and shisha pipes. I spotted a stash of booze on the coffee table and helped myself, while Amanda walked over to a guy sat in an armchair in the corner. I guessed she knew him so I left her to it until, taking a sip of my drink, I saw her heading back over to me.

'Sammy, I'll be back in ten minutes,' she told me, looking back at the man she'd been talking to.

'Okay,' I replied, not asking where she was going. The pair of them exited the room, leaving me on my own. Not that I minded. I was tipsy enough to make conversation with anyone and the men were all so nice to me, making the effort to talk to me.

'Are you having a good night?' asked a man sat on the couch, and I nodded. Everyone at the party seemed to be attracted to me and they all wanted to talk to me when I walked past them. It felt like I'd won a popularity contest. When I wandered into the kitchen, one guy came up to me. Like most of the men at the party he was Asian but he looked a lot younger than the others, perhaps in his late twenties.

'Hey, hon.' He smiled at me. 'What've you been up to today?'

'Just some shoplifting,' I replied. The vodka had started to go to my head and I danced along with the music as I talked.

'Nice', he remarked, placing his hand on my childlike bum. At first it didn't bother me; instead I quite liked the attention. He fancies me, I thought, and I had a fluttery feeling in my stomach. 'What are you taking?' he added.

'Weed,' I answered. His hand was sliding lower and lower until it was under my skirt. Starting to feel uncomfortable, I tried to wriggle myself free but he pulled me in closer.

'What are you doing?' I asked, squirming while his other arm held me tightly.

'Relax,' he whispered. Without warning, he forced his hand in between my bum cheeks, as though he was reaching for my bumhole. Shocked, I immediately pushed him away.

'Get off me now,' I shouted at him. 'Don't come near me.' I waited for the other men to stick up for me. I was so much smaller than him, and I was sure the rest of them would take a young girl's side over him, but they didn't move. Instead, they just watched, looking bemused.

'What the fuck?' The guy started to argue, but at that moment Amanda marched into the room, pulling me away from him.

# AMANDA

'Are you okay?' she asked, so I told her what had happened. 'That's awful, Sammy, come on, let's leave.' I was upset but glad to have Amanda by my side.

'It was just one creep,' she reassured me once we were back at hers. 'They're not all like that.' Not wanting to let it ruin our fun, I put it down to one bad experience, but in the back of my mind I was worried it would happen again. Amanda offered to take me to more parties and I agreed. And it started to become a way of life.

'You're wild,' Amanda would comment, laughing at my drunken dancing at the parties. I loved getting drunk with her, and there was always free weed and vodka wherever we went. One night, I sat on a sofa in a random house Amanda had taken me to. She had wandered off again, promising to be back soon, and, having a large swig of my drink, I thought back to my dad's lecture years ago. You're wrong, Dad, I said to myself, there's plenty of free things in this world. I thought the men let me have free weed and alcohol because I was cool. They must love me, I thought, scanning the room and all the faces staring back at me. To me, Amanda and I were an untouchable duo and everyone wanted to be our friend.

Meanwhile I still hated my foster house in Shiregreen, taking every chance I could to be anywhere else. David had been missing from his children's home for a couple of days and, after I spotted him in town, he led me to his secret hideout.

'Hold on.' David motioned with his hand to stop. 'Look,

there's a camera.' We were beside a row of abandoned garages on a secluded street about a mile from my foster home. After waiting for the security camera to rotate, David sprinted to the garage on the end and lifted the metal shutter slightly.

'Come on, hurry up,' he urged, and I ran to follow him. Once inside, David lit some candles and I marvelled at his hidden home.

'Do you like my shed?' he asked, gesturing to the random items of derelict furniture.

'Wow, is this where you're living?' I asked. Inside there was a single mattress on the floor lying next to broken chairs and a dresser.

'Yeah,' David replied, as he continued to light the room with candles he'd stolen from Wilko. 'I found it with Chloe.' Chloe was a girl I knew from around our area. We'd never really spoken before but I knew she was friends with David.

'That's great.' I tried to smile, envious of the freedom they had there.

'You can live here too if you want,' he offered, almost sensing what I was thinking.

'Really?' The thought of having a secret place where no one, not even social services, could find me sounded like heaven.

'Of course,' he confirmed. 'I need you to help me make it nice.'

The pair of us tried our best to make the shed homely. We robbed bedding from TK Maxx and kitted it out with a dressing table and mirror and anything else we could find at the local tip. The shed was dim at night so we nicked plenty more candles from a nearby church and, before long, I considered it to be my home. Chloe and I were the same age and, both hating our foster homes, we stuck together. I'd sit outside the corner shop, waiting for someone to buy booze for me before taking it back to the shed to drink with Chloe. When we were desperate we'd nip back to our foster homes for a shower and some food, then it was back to the shed to sleep.

After getting caught shoplifting by police I had been put on an electronic tag but I didn't care if I broke my curfew. Instead, I started going drinking with Amanda nearly every night. I was scrawny, and I still hadn't hit puberty yet, but I strolled into the parties like I owned the place.

'Alright, boys?' I asked confidently, swinging my arm around Amanda's shoulder. We hadn't been to a house party in that particular area before but I recognised some of the faces that stared back at me. One thing all of the houses had in common was that none of them looked lived in. There were no paintings or family pictures on the walls, and nothing but beer stocked in the fridge. It was as if these houses were strictly for parties. Seeing the creepy way the men looked me up and down would have intimidated me if it weren't for Amanda. Having her there gave me a sense of security. I could drink and smoke as much as I wanted to and nothing bad could happen to me because my best friend would protect me. I got so drunk that I danced around the living room, even though there wasn't any music.

I heard someone say, 'Hey baby.' A guy came up to me and I flashed him a smile.

'Hiya,' I replied, still dancing.

'How much?' he asked, and I frowned, confused by what he'd said.

'Eh?' I replied, convinced I must have heard him wrong. 'How much what?' But before he could respond, Amanda moved herself in between us, taking my hand to dance with me. I felt euphoric. We were a little team. There were times when the guys would get rowdy, grabbing my bum or chest, but Amanda always stuck up for me, shouting at them to get off me. She was more than my friend, she was like a sister, and I felt I could always depend on her.

Being friends with Amanda made me feel pressured to lose my virginity, though. All she talked about was sex and, while I didn't feel ready to do it myself yet, I knew I couldn't keep telling her the same story without her getting suspicious. We'd pace around town, arm in arm, laughing and making fun of people we saw. She'd update me on her latest conquests and I'd pretend I was seeing someone. I knew she had a boyfriend called Spencer because she talked about him, but that didn't stop her from chasing after every other boy in Sheffield.

When she wasn't flirting with men at the markets, Amanda would be flashing the cash. She always seemed to have a lot of money and every time I met up with her she was in a brand new outfit. Like every other care kid, Amanda received a clothing grant, but I knew even that wouldn't cover all the things she owned. Not that I ever dared to ask her where she got the money from. Amanda gave off a sense of authority and what she said went. I guessed her boyfriend had perhaps bought her clothes as presents. If anything, I envied her wardrobe and, just like I wished I could be more like her, I also desperately wanted the kind of money that would buy me her clothes.

One day I was out looking for her when I spotted Olivia, Amanda's friend, in town. She was sat on the steps near the markets and, after giving her a wave, I walked over. I didn't like Olivia; the few times I had met her there had been a competitive tension between us over Amanda, but that day I approached her hoping she'd seen her.

'Alright?' I began. 'Do you know where Amanda is?'

'No, I've not seen her but do you always have to be joined to Amanda's hip?' Olivia snapped at me. 'She's not your best mate.'

'Yes she is,' I argued back. I had always been jealous of Olivia's friendship with Amanda but there was no way she was closer to her than I was. 'Amanda's my best friend.'

Olivia let out a forced laugh.

'If you love her so much then how come you don't know what she is?' Olivia prodded. 'You're just a little girl.'

'I know everything about Amanda,' I retorted. I hated Olivia in that moment. 'We tell each other everything.'

'I bet she hasn't told you this,' she shouted. 'Amanda's a prostitute.'

'What's a prostitute?' I asked, confused as to what Olivia was getting at.

'She has sex for money,' she replied bluntly.

'No way,' I blurted out. 'You're lying.' I couldn't believe what she was telling me. I stormed off, not wanting to listen to her any longer.

I wanted to think Olivia was a liar but, after our row, I couldn't stop thinking about what she'd said. Is that where Amanda gets all her money from? I wondered. I tried to shake the thought from my mind but I couldn't and, that evening, I sat in Amanda's bedroom, pressuring her to tell me.

'I just don't get it,' I pressed, not believing her excuses. 'You have so much money, it has to be from somewhere.'

'People buy me things, what's the big deal?' Amanda scoffed. She was refusing to look me in the eye and I could tell I'd touched a nerve.

'What people?' I persisted. 'And that doesn't explain why you always have so much money.'

'Fine.' Amanda gave in with an audible sigh. 'I have sex for money, is that what you wanted to know? But look at all the things I have.' She gestured at all the stuff in her room.

'That's gross!' I exclaimed, shocked at her confession. 'How can you do that?'

'It's easy.' Amanda shrugged. 'It's just sex. You've had sex before.'

'Obviously.' I gulped, not wanting to admit the truth. 'But those men are *so old*.' Amanda rolled her eyes at me.

'Grow up, Sammy, it's nothing,' she insisted. 'You can do it too, you know.'

'I don't think I could–' I started to say, before she interrupted me.

'Of course you can. You could make up to two hundred pounds from a guy, depending on what you do,' Amanda continued, pausing to look at me. 'You're so young, Sammy, and the younger you are, the more money you get.' I didn't know what to think but the promise of money made it almost sound like a good idea – but not quite.

'I don't think I could do that for money,' I resolved out loud, thinking back to my fantasy of losing my virginity on the beach.

'You know what, I thought you were cool, Sammy.' Amanda's words were cutting. 'Was I wrong?'

I didn't know what to say. Amanda was like my sister. I spent every day with her. I styled myself to look like her. I knew if I went against her on this then I'd effectively be cutting her from my life and that wasn't something I could do. Having sex for money with men old enough to be my dad sounded disgusting but Amanda was getting a nice lifestyle in return. Eventually I spoke up.

'No, you're not wrong.' I chose my words carefully. 'It's up to you.'

'Next time we go to a party, I can show you,' she offered. 'It's not as scary as it sounds.'

'Okay,' I replied, just to appease her. If she ever asks me to do it I'll just say I'm busy, I resolved to myself. The thought of sleeping with the men at the parties terrified me and there was no chance I'd actually go through with it. But a few days later I was back in Amanda's room when she handed me a pair of jeans and a top.

'That's for Friday night,' she informed me, and I felt my heart sink. 'I'll meet you beforehand.'

I wanted to scream, 'I'm not doing it. There's no way!' But at that point it was like I went onto autopilot and convinced myself I'd think of an excuse before the party: I'm sick, I've been arrested, I have a boyfriend . . . the hopeless excuses ran through my mind for days. I'm a virgin, I thought. That was one thing I definitely couldn't tell her.

By Friday I knew there wasn't a way out. That day I sat in the shed drinking with Chloe. I hadn't told her what I was planning to do that night but I think she could sense from my silence that something wasn't right. I thought it would be easier if I was off my face before I got there, so swigging my two-litre bottle of cider, I willed myself to get drunk. The day seemed to whizz by, and when I checked my phone for the time I saw it was ten to five. *Shit*. I was meeting Amanda at 5 p.m., so I needed to leave. Scared to move, I took one more gulp of cider before stuffing the bottle into my rucksack. It's now or never, I told myself. Zipping up my bag, I felt my hands start to shake a little as the nerves set in.

'Right, I'm off out,' I announced to Chloe, who was lying

on the mattress, typing away on her flip phone. 'See you later.' I hoped she'd wonder where I was going, or ask me to stay, but she didn't.

'Yeah, laters,' Chloe replied, looking up briefly to give me a quick smile before returning to her phone. I guess I actually have to go now, I thought, reminding my legs that they needed to move.

I wandered down the path from my shed to the subways where I was due to meet Amanda. The subways consisted of four tunnels connecting to different parts of Sheffield and, when I got there, I could see Amanda already waiting for me, standing by the entrance.

'You ready to go?' she asked. I'd had so much to drink I could barely walk, but Amanda looked completely sober.

'Yeah, course,' I replied, but inside I wanted to throw up. Amanda started to head through the tunnel and I followed her, the uneven gravel tripping me up as I went. Peering back at the path behind me, I desperately wanted to run back to the safety of the shed, but I couldn't. Instead, I walked on with Amanda, each weighted step feeling like a pull closer into danger.

# 5.

# GROOMED

In a drunken daze, I followed Amanda through the tunnels in Shiregreen until I no longer knew where we were.

'So, where's the party?' I asked tentatively, trailing a few feet behind her.

'We're going to Spencer's first,' she replied. Although I'd seen the often-spoken-of boyfriend with her a couple of times, he'd always been kept at arm's length. I never questioned it, though, as I preferred it when I didn't have to compete for Amanda's attention.

'Oh, okay,' I mumbled, confused as to why we had to go there first. 'How come?'

'We need to get that tag off you,' she insisted, looking down at the electronic band wrapped around my ankle. 'They won't be happy if they see that.'

'Right,' I answered, but by that point I wasn't really listening. I was too busy focusing on putting one foot in front of the other. Wandering through the subway tunnels, Amanda led us to Spencer's place. He worked as a mechanic in a garage and had his own flat nearby. He'd know how to get the tag off.

The walk to Spencer's house had sobered me up, and by the time I sat down on his kitchen floor I didn't feel drunk at all. Spencer was the same age as Amanda, and he seemed to know what she got up to, but if it bothered him he never let on. Clutching a pair of pliers, he forced the electronic band off my ankle.

'You're free,' he laughed, dangling the tag above my face. I smirked as I scrambled to my feet but, inside, my stomach twisted into knots. I don't feel free, I thought. I looked around the kitchen in search of something strong to drink.

'Have you got any booze?' I asked Spencer, but he just looked at Amanda, waiting for her to respond.

'Not here, Sammy,' Amanda said dismissively. 'We should get going.' I sighed. I wanted to stay longer, thinking of any excuse to put off the inevitable, but it was no use. Now that the tag was off, Amanda wanted to go and, as she got up to leave, I had no choice but to follow.

'Okay,' I agreed, defeated. 'See you later, then.' Spencer waved us out the door and Amanda led me back down the street.

'Where's the party?' I asked her again, stroking the goosebumps on my arms. It was late October and, while my beer coat had been keeping me warm, I was now starting to feel the breeze.

'About ten minutes away,' she replied. 'We'll be there soon.' The pink flowery top Amanda had told me to wear clung to me uncomfortably. I tugged at my clothes, trying to stretch them out. I'd matched the top with light-blue jeans and, in an attempt to look older, I'd dabbed glittery eyeshadow over my eyelids. I'm too sober for this, I thought, and started to panic. I need to get drunk, fast. Desperate, I spotted a pub down the road and ran over to their beer garden at the front. There were a few leftover pints on the tables, so I swiped them.

'Waste not, want not,' I joked to Amanda, lifting my free pint towards her before downing it. Amanda chuckled and nabbed a glass for herself. I hoped she would forget about the party but, after chugging a couple of pints, Amanda was keen to move on.

'Come on,' she ordered, giving my arm a tug. 'We need to go.'

'I wish we had a bottle of vodka,' I suggested, as we set off again. Amanda smiled but didn't say anything back and I spent the rest of the time trailing a few feet behind her, watching the wind blow through the trees above us. The walk may have only been ten minutes but it felt like forever. Finally we reached Godric Road and I followed Amanda until she stopped outside a house. Three steps with chipped red paint led up to the door. Each small step took an eternity to climb. Amanda rang the bell before stepping back behind me. After a few seconds, an Asian man answered the door. He towered over us with a blokeish demeanour and looked like he was at least thirty.

'Hi,' he grunted, gripping the door. His expression was blank and, as he looked down at what I was wearing, I crossed my arms uncomfortably and turned back to Amanda. I gasped, realising she was leaving and, frightened by the man, I grabbed onto the back of her shirt.

'Where are we going?' I whispered to her. 'Are we not going to the party?' I glanced back to see the man watching us, impatient.

'Oh, no,' Amanda said, shaking herself free from my grip. 'You're staying here.' My stomach dropped.

'Why are you leaving then?' I gave her a wide-eyed stare. Don't leave me, I pleaded internally. If you go now I'll never speak to you again.

'You want vodka, don't you?' she scoffed, shrugging. 'I'll be back in a minute.' From the doorstep I could hear other men laughing and talking inside.

'Who's in there, then?' I asked her, pointing to the door. My heart raced. It felt like time was passing so slowly.

'They'll tell you where to go,' Amanda said, and gave me a shove towards the man. 'You'll be fine.' Giving me one last look, she turned on her heels and left. I stood there, rooted to the spot, watching her walk away until she was out of sight. *She's not really leaving me, is she?* I couldn't believe what was happening but when I realised Amanda wasn't coming back for me, I had no choice but to turn around and face the guy.

'Come in.' He ushered me through the door and led me towards the living room. It looked like a house that had been converted into flats and we were on the ground floor. Usually when I entered parties I was really confident because I had Amanda with me, but this time was different. With my head ducked down, I peered around, mostly noticing the feet of men walking in and out.

The living room was filthy, with layers of grime and mould coating the walls. There were a few men sat around sharing a hashish pipe. I lingered in the doorway, watching them. This was different from any other party, as there was no music or dancing, and while the houses were usually packed with people, there were just five men in this house and no girls in sight. Resting against the back wall was a long, brown leather sofa and I made a beeline for it. There was no one on the sofa but, nervous as hell, I perched myself on the arm, not wanting to take up too much room.

I couldn't help but notice that as I'd moved to sit down, all of the men in the room had turned to stare at me. I could feel myself going red, glancing up to see that they were still looking. Why is it so hot? I thought. I need to calm down. My cheeks burned as I reached for the cider in my bag and realised there was only a bit left. I finished it off as I looked at the TV blaring in the corner. The six o'clock news was on and I immediately started to sweat. I'm a missing child, I thought, panicked. What if I'm on the news? Deep down I knew it was irrational, but all rational thought had long gone out the window and I couldn't bear the idea of what would happen if the men got angry with me. I wish this news would just shut up, I thought to myself.

After a few minutes, one of the men got up and walked towards me. Like the others he was Asian and looked to be in his late twenties or early thirties.

'Come on, then.' He beckoned at me to follow him. I rose from the couch and he escorted me to a bedroom at the front of the house. In total desperation I convinced myself that Amanda would be in the room, and my face fell when I realised she wasn't there.

'Do you mind if I have a fag?' I asked, as the man shut the bedroom door.

'No, go ahead,' he replied in a thick foreign accent, and sat himself down on the bed. I cracked open the window, lit a cigarette and leant out to smoke it. I could smell the fresh air and it was starting to hit me just how scary this house was. It didn't feel like a party at all. I knew why I was there.

*Where the fuck are you?* I wondered, wishing Amanda could telepathically hear me. *Get here now.* I couldn't understand why she'd leave me alone in this place. Anger started to rise up within me, tears pricking the corners of my eyes. I can't be seen crying, I thought. I don't want them to think I'm weak.

Staring out of the window at the road outside, I took deep breaths, trying to relax. I wondered over and over again where Amanda was, praying she'd magically reappear, but she was nowhere to be seen. I finished my cigarette but couldn't remember having taken a single drag of it. It was as if it had blown away in the wind.

With nothing else to distract me from what was happening, I had no choice but to turn around and face the man. He was still slouched on the bed but he had taken off his trousers and was looking at me expectantly. I resigned myself to the fact that I just needed to get this over with, petrified of what was coming. Pushing my fears to the back of my mind, I sat myself down and kissed him. I instantly regretted it. Shit, I thought. I've started it. I can't stop now.

He grabbed at my hair, trying to drag my head towards his crotch, but I wriggled free. His penis looked dirty and I felt sick at the thought of having to touch it or have it near my face. *I'd rather he pinned me down than I had to do that.* No sooner had the notion entered my mind than he seized me by the arms and threw me down onto the bed. He crawled on top of me, his weight crushing down on my tiny frame.

I tried to convince myself it was my choice, that I wanted to do this, but no matter how much I repeated it I couldn't persuade my body to respond. Instead, I wriggled uncomfortably underneath him, struggling to catch my breath. He fiddled with my zip and pulled my jeans down to my ankles. I lay back down, and he forced himself inside me. I was so small that he tore me and I lay with my eyes squeezed shut as the excruciating pain coursed through me.

'Look at me,' he ordered, pulling my hands away from my eyes. I did as I was asked, looking him in the eyes as I put my arms around him. Running my fingers down his back, I felt a cross-shaped scar on his shoulder blade. He stopped me abruptly.

'No,' he barked, pulling my hands away from him. After that, I made a point not to touch him at all. I lay as still as a corpse, with my arms by my side, thinking of anything but what was happening. I might steal some more candles from the shop tomorrow, I thought, as he raped me. They'd look nice in the shed.

He tried to pull my top up but I shoved it back down. He looked annoyed, dragging the shirt up harder. There's nothing to see anyway, I thought to myself. I hadn't hit puberty yet and I didn't even need to wear a bra. But he forced the top up to my shoulders, exposing my childish cropped vest. He grabbed at the flat skin on my chest and I think he liked the fact that I didn't have breasts.

When he was finished, he rolled over and looked down at the sheets. There was a pool of blood stretching underneath my thighs.

'You filthy, filthy girl,' he tutted, doing up his trousers before he left the room. My face was red hot with embarrassment and I curled my legs inwards. I hadn't even started my first period yet and the thought of everyone laughing at me in the other room made me want to cry. I remained on the bed for a long time after, scared to move in case they shouted at me. But after a while I realised I was desperate for a wee. Will they mind me using the toilet? I wondered, as I crept out of the bedroom.

Sneaking down the hallway to the bathroom, I could hear

the men talking in another language in the living room. If they heard me, they didn't bother to follow. Once in the bathroom, I hovered over the toilet and let out a small scream. Having a wee was agony. My hands were shaking as I tried to wipe myself but my crotch stung so painfully that it hurt too much to touch.

After that I wandered into the kitchen at the back of the house, where I found a packet of chocolate biscuits on the dining table. Without thinking I sat myself down and started to eat them. I'm starving, I realised, devouring the packet. I wondered when I'd be allowed to leave. I was missing the familiarity of our shed when, without warning, there was a sharp knock at the door. I jumped. Maybe it's Amanda, I hoped, listening carefully as one of the men left the living room to answer it. But it was another man who entered the house; I could hear his rough voice in the hallway. I couldn't make out what they were saying but, as the pair of them walked into the kitchen, I panicked and, terrified, I bowed my head, not wanting to look at them.

'No,' I heard the visitor yell upon stepping into the room. 'She's too old.' I cowered in my seat, staring down at the table. I waited for them to leave, listening to the front door slam before peering up. I was alone again.

With nowhere else to go, I headed back to the bathroom where I stood staring at myself in the mirror. I'm too sober, I thought. I need a drink. I let the tap run, cupping my hands to catch the water before putting it to my mouth. That was a shot of vodka, I thought to myself, before taking another gulp of water. That was another one. I tried to pretend I was getting tipsy, wishing I was anywhere but there. I heard a laugh coming from the living room and it made me shiver. *I don't want to be here anymore.*

Stepping out into the hallway, I saw the living room door was ajar, and facing it was the front door. I crept over to the living room door and took a deep breath before legging it to get to the front door. As soon as I stepped outside I bolted, running for my life down the street. I didn't know I could run so fast, as I sprinted down the dark road, refusing to look back. I didn't want to know if anyone was following me and, not wanting to turn around to find out, I didn't stop running until I was back at the shed. When I got there I was relieved to discover I was alone. I lay on the small mattress and clutched my stomach as it ached, willing the night to end.

The next morning I awoke to find David top-and-tailing next to me. At first I smiled at the sight of a familiar face, but a pang of pain hit the bottom of my stomach and I groaned.

'Where were you last night?' David croaked, peeking at me with one eye open.

'Just out,' I replied, struggling to get to my feet. Not wanting David to ask any more questions, I quickly got dressed and left.

I caught the bus and headed into town in search of Amanda. It didn't take me long to find her stood smoking outside Bargain Booze near the markets. As always, a crowd of men surrounded her but, clocking me as I approached her, she nodded and pulled me away to one side.

'How was it?' she asked, taking a drag of her cigarette. I had built up a speech of what I wanted to say, but now that I was standing in front of her my mind went blank.

'Easy as piss,' I lied, feeling the need to brag. 'I can't wait for next time.' Oh God, why did I say that? I thought, but Amanda was ecstatic.

'Well done,' she praised, giving me a slap on the back. 'I'm proud of you.' She handed me one of her fags and I lit it.

'Where were you last night, then?' I questioned, still angry that she'd left me on my own.

'I got sidetracked,' she replied and I just nodded. I know you're lying, I seethed, but there was no point in arguing with her.

'Right, fair enough,' I retorted. 'I didn't need you anyway.' The last thing I wanted was for her to think I was vulnerable.

'Good,' Amanda answered, before gesturing towards a row of shops. 'Anyway, we've got a spending spree to go on.' With that, she led me round different stores, treating me to new clothes as a reward for the night before. I took a shine to a pair of Tatty Teddy socks and I was over the moon when she bought them for me. The pair of us had a great day, laughing together, and I'd almost forgotten the events of the previous night until she brought it up again.

'You know, you can do this all the time if you want,' she suggested. We were sat in McDonald's after she'd bought me my tea. 'And you can have so many nice things.' I took a sip of my Coke, mulling over what to say.

'Yeah, I know,' I eventually replied. 'The clothes are really nice.' I did envy Amanda's lifestyle but my belly was aching, still sore from the awful night, and I couldn't imagine going through it again.

'There's another party we can go to tomorrow,' she told me. 'It's right cool and there's money in it for you.'

'Oh,' I replied, and there was suddenly a knot in the pit of my stomach. 'Okay then.' I desperately wanted to avoid Amanda's parties but I was scared she wouldn't want to be my friend anymore.

'So you'll come with me?' she asked, not breaking eye contact. She posed it as a question but I knew deep down I didn't really have a choice.

'Will you be there with me this time?' I responded. I didn't want to be left alone again and Amanda nodded her head.

'Yeah, course,' she replied. 'It'll be a laugh.'

'Fine.' I felt backed into a corner and I didn't want to let Amanda down.

'Good girl. There's plenty more where this came from,' she said, grinning and pointing at the clothes bags beside me, and I beamed back at her.

'I can't wait.' I giggled, thinking of all the nice things I'd be able to buy next. In that moment, I thought I had some kind of control over the situation. I figured that because I was getting some clothes and money out of it, it was okay for Amanda to send me to houses to be abused by groups of older men. To me, that seemed like a fair trade. I didn't have a clue about what I'd been sucked into. At the naive and impressionable age of thirteen, I had no idea that I had been well and truly groomed by my best friend.

# 6.

# TRAFFICKED

'Don't forget to meet me later on Infirmary Road', Amanda reminded me over text. I huffed, chucking my phone to one side. *How could I forget? I'm dreading it.* It was the day of the next party and I found myself alone, lying on the mattress in the shed. I stroked my belly absentmindedly; it was still hurting from the other night and I wondered if there was a way to get out of going to this new party. It was as if I had a stitch in the pit of my stomach that wouldn't go away. I thought back to how I'd imagined sex to be, like the movies I'd seen growing up, full of love and romance. *Wow, what a massive disappointment.*

'Hey, Sammy.' David poked his head round the garage door before climbing through the gap. 'What've you been up to?'

'Not much,' I mumbled, not wanting to tell him the truth.

# PIMPED

The closer Amanda and I had become, the further apart David and I had grown.

'Well, if you're not doing anything,' he continued, plonking himself down on the floor beside me, 'I'm going to a party down Infirmary Road tonight if you want to join.'

Suddenly my ears pricked up. He couldn't possibly be talking about the same party.

'Infirmary Road?' I repeated, trying to hide the panic in my voice.

'Yeah,' David continued. 'It's at my mate's flat.' I breathed a sigh of relief. There was no way David knew anyone running the kind of parties Amanda went to.

'Yeah, sure,' I agreed, glad of the distraction. 'I'll come with you.'

That night I headed to a block of flats in Upperthorpe and my heart raced as it dawned on me that Amanda was waiting just a few floors below at a different flat. Don't think about it, I told myself, trying to brush off the thought of what would be expected of me later that night.

Once there, David left me to mingle with friends, so I wandered around in search of booze. This is such a strange party, I noted, the atmosphere being very different to any of the houses Amanda had taken me to. I looked around at all the boys and girls roughly my age, dancing and laughing together, and it suddenly dawned on me: this was the first real party I'd ever been to. I started to relax, and I was having such a good time that I didn't want the night to end, but my heart sank when I felt my phone buzz.

'Hey, are you coming?' Amanda wrote, and I sighed. For a split second I considered ignoring the message but I knew I couldn't keep her waiting. I reluctantly set about preparing to leave. Swiping any booze I could find lying around the kitchen, I filled my bag with bottles before heading to another flat downstairs. I didn't know how Amanda always seemed to know exactly where these parties were, directing me where to go, but I didn't question it. I knocked on the door, holding my breath, waiting a couple of seconds before she answered.

'Hey!' Amanda exclaimed, drunkenly. 'Come join the fun.' She ushered me into the flat and I looked around: it was a far cry from the party I'd just left. The place was a bedsit, just one small room with a musty couch leaning against the wall and a tiny bed in the corner – and it was filthy. The only other room was the poxy bathroom on the other side of the flat. As I followed Amanda towards the sofa, I nodded a hello to the two men in the room.

Some party this is, I groaned to myself. I'd been having so much fun just beforehand and I wished I could be back upstairs. The bedsit was completely bare, as though no one really lived there. There isn't even a kettle, I thought. That's so weird.

I looked over at the men drinking with Amanda. There was a big age difference between the two of them, the older one being short and skinny, and at least fifty. Doing a double take, I immediately recognised the older man as 'Charlie', a middle-aged Asian guy I'd seen paying Mum the occasional visit while I'd been round at hers. He had a massive silver car that he sometimes took her shopping in, and I'd even once gone out for the day with him when he'd escorted the kids to the park. My eyes lit up. I've got you, Charlie, I thought with glee. I've got your cards.

I took my spot in a small wooden chair next to the couch, my stare burning a hole into the side of Charlie's face. He glared back at me and, by the scared look in his eyes, I could tell he wasn't happy to see me but neither of us let on that we knew each other. Instead, and without a word, I pulled a bottle of Bacardi from my rucksack and sipped it, listening to Amanda talk drunken nonsense to the men.

'I've converted to Islam,' she announced to the room, her arms flailing dramatically. 'I'm a Muslim.' I rolled my eyes but, taking another swig from my bottle, I didn't let Charlie out of my sight. He shifted uncomfortably, not wanting to meet my gaze. If you even try anything with me, I thought, smirking to myself, I'll tell my mum exactly what you are. I rolled myself a joint and lit it.

'It's Eid, right?' Amanda continued. I watched the younger man nod at her question as I sat silently to one side. Time passed and, as neither of the men had initiated anything sexual, I started to relax, thinking I'd get away with not having to do anything with them.

'I'm just going to the toilet,' I excused myself, not that anyone was paying attention to me. Sat in the bathroom, I considered the ways I could make my exit to head back to the party upstairs. I don't think they even want me here, I pondered. Hopefully they won't care if I just leave. I made my way back into the main room and I was stunned. In the five minutes I'd been gone, Amanda had undone Charlie's jeans and her head was now in his crotch. Unsure of what to do, I slowly sat back down in my chair. I saw that Amanda was glancing at me out of the corner of her eye, and the weight of pressure mounted. I knew I'd have to instigate something with the other guy who was looking at me from his seat on the sofa next to Charlie and Amanda. At least it's not Charlie, I thought, before leaning over to kiss him.

This time didn't feel as scary as the last. Amanda was there and she was my best friend – she wasn't going to let anything bad happen to me. I felt confident and, not wanting to let her down, I instead wanted to show off how grown up I was. The guy I was kissing wasn't completely gross to look at but I still wasn't attracted to him and, as he started to pull his trousers down, I was more focused on what Amanda and Charlie were doing.

Out of nowhere, though, this guy grabbed me and forced me onto the floor. I lay still as he raped me on the floorboards, thinking over and over again how proud Amanda would be of me. He was less aggressive than the first guy, holding my sides and kissing my neck, but it hurt all the same. As my crotch stung, I was petrified I'd bleed again. That would be so cringey. This guy made leering comments about how smooth my skin was, and I blushed, embarrassed. I was still too young to have much hair down there. I ignored what he was saying and looked back over to Amanda and Charlie. Watching them instead, I willed this nightmare to end.

Afterwards he didn't speak to me but went back to sit on the sofa, lighting himself a cigarette. I quickly got myself dressed, hovering around, debating whether I should ask for money. But I felt too embarrassed. Amanda will sort that out for me, I conceded. She was still having sex with Charlie in the corner but I was desperate to leave.

'Um,' I awkwardly announced, gravitating towards the door. 'I'll see you later, Amanda.' She stopped what she was doing and peered up to wave at me.

'Laters, Sammy.'

Leaving her there, I strolled back up to the party that was still in full swing upstairs. Upon re-entering the flat, it was strange, as if the previous hour downstairs had never happened. Suddenly I was back to being a normal thirteen-year-old girl again. I spotted David in the living room and marched over to him.

'Hiya.' He grinned, giving me a fist bump. 'Where have you been?'

'Just about,' I responded vaguely. David was too drunk to notice I was clutching my belly in pain.

The atmosphere of the party was electric and I even met a teenage boy who went by the name of Flex. He was the same age as me and at the end of the night he put his number into my phone.

'Text me sometime,' Flex told me as he left and I smiled, butterflies jittering around my stomach.

'Yeah, definitely,' I replied. It was exciting to encounter someone my age who was interested in me for a change. Flex and I did meet up a couple of times after that, and once we even kissed behind the cinema after David had got us kicked out. The innocence of our dates was what I had longed for but it would never have lasted – I was going on jobs for Amanda nearly every day and that took up all of my attention.

All of the days were starting to blur into one. I was sore all of the time, so I got as drunk as I could to mask the pain. I'd get so intoxicated that it wouldn't be until the next morning that the pain would hit me like a ton of bricks and I'd writhe in agony on the shed mattress, wondering what had happened to me the night before. A lot of the time I was too drunk to remember what was happening but there were some nights I wished I could forget.

One evening Amanda dragged me to a house where a man in his fifties took a shine to me. He was a skinny Asian man with a weird fringe and, leading me into the bedroom, he insisted that I called him 'Daddy'.

'Kiss Daddy on the lips,' he leered, as he sat me down on the bed. I hated it but I knew I had to do it. He ordered me onto my knees and I gave him a blowjob. As always, my mind wandered to nicer things. How great would it be to get a puppy? I thought. I wonder if I could get one for the shed . . . I was preoccupied in blocking out reality when, without warning, he slapped me hard across the face.

'Look Daddy in the eye,' he insisted, and clutching my bruised cheek he pulled at my skin until I looked at him. All I wanted was to glance away, not wanting to see his evil face, but I was too afraid he'd hit me again. After that I developed a complex about eye contact, too uncomfortable to look at anyone directly.

Sometimes I'd begin to feel in control of what was happening at the parties, convincing myself that I was in charge, but then an incident would occur to remind me just how vulnerable I was.

'How old are you?' one guy asked me. He had pinned me down on the bedroom floor of a random house Amanda had sent me to. I grimaced as he touched himself while he lay on top of me. As whenever anyone asked my age, I gave him the same answer.

'Sixteen,' I muttered. His ugly face was inches away from mine and I squirmed, trying to look anywhere but directly at him.

'Liar,' he sneered, smiling and grabbing at the cup of my bra. I still had no breasts to fill it but Amanda had given it to me to wear. 'I know you're not sixteen.' I noticed a spider running along the wall and I followed it with my eyes, envying its escape.

'Right,' I admitted without looking at him. 'I'm thirteen.' I didn't know what difference it would make knowing my real age but the man still wasn't satisfied with my answer and he grabbed me by the shoulders.

'No you're not,' he protested. 'You're younger.' I turned to stare back at him. Fuck it, I decided. If this is what it takes to make you hurry up, I'll do it.

'I'm eleven,' I lied, and his evil grin made me feel sick. I knew he thrived off the idea of me being young. Paedophile, I thought to myself, as he raped me.

A few days later I found myself trapped in a similar situation, lying on the bathroom floor of another house. I really hadn't wanted to have sex with this particular man – he was ugly and brutish – but Amanda had nudged me towards him and I did as I was told.

I was still outwardly fearless to the men who approached me, blindly believing Amanda would stick up for me if anything went drastically wrong. Many of the men were rough with me, and I'd grown to expect it, but this man in the bathroom was much worse. As he raped me, he punched the floor next to my head. His fist was so close that I could feel his knuckles graze my ear as they smacked the floor with a thud. Scared, I lay frozen, terrified to move in case he hurt me. He thumped the floor over and over again, and each time I winced as his hand moved closer. My crotch tore and I knew I would be in agony for days. Afterwards I curled up alone on the laminate floor, dabbing the tears from the corners of my eyes. What the fuck was that? I asked myself as I cried. Why was he so horrible?

I never dared ask for money from any of the men. It was always Amanda who paid me. She'd pass on fifty or sixty quid here and there, or take me on shopping trips as payment for doing her bidding. Amanda and I still spent the daytime lingering around the markets, cadging fags from the groups of men who surrounded us. I recognised some of them from the parties but they never let on that they knew me.

'Ew, look at her,' said Amanda one day, nodding to a frumpy woman juggling her shopping bags. 'Ugly cow.' We were people-watching as we smoked outside the bookies.

'Yeah, what the fuck is she wearing?' I replied, not really taking in which woman Amanda was talking about. While I had to endure the evenings spent with random men, I lived for the shopping sprees Amanda and I went on during the day, giggling as we tried on shimmery tops in New Look. I wished our time together was always this fun. The pair of us had such a laugh and I felt so cool being her friend. Everyone knew who Amanda was and, when I was with her, they knew me too.

When I was younger, I had always been a lonely little girl, constantly being bullied or terrorised by other kids, but now, for the first time, I was popular. In my mind, all the people at the parties were my friends and they wanted me there because I was cool like Amanda. What I was made to do at the various houses wasn't a part of being Amanda's friend that I enjoyed, but it was something I was learning to accept.

A few months later, I turned fourteen and started my period. Amanda was the only one I could confide in and she took me to buy pads and tampons, telling me through the door of a toilet cubicle how to use them. When I started to grow pubic hair, Amanda taught me how to shave, picking up razors for me to use. It was just like having a big sister.

Amanda turned sixteen around this time, which meant she was now officially a care leaver. No longer allowed to stay at her children's home, she was moved into a B&B behind London Street, near the centre of Sheffield. I was so jealous that she was leaving care as it made her even cooler in my eyes.

'You can come live with me if you want to,' Amanda offered, bigging it up as a lavish life in a hotel suite. 'It'll be awesome.'

'Seriously?' I asked, surprised but delighted. 'I'd love to.' I couldn't believe it. I was still making trips back to my foster home every couple of days for a shower, so the prospect of upgrading from the cold shed where I spent most nights to a posh hotel was exciting, but when we got there the B&B staff weren't happy with my presence.

'Can't my sister stay?' Amanda argued with the receptionist, but she shook her head.

'No, she can't,' she disagreed. 'Your social worker has only paid for *you* to stay here.'

'Okay, fair enough.' Amanda appeared to give in, but once we were out of sight she rushed me up the stairs to her room. I couldn't wait for a break from kipping in the shed but I quickly realised Amanda's living situation wasn't all it was cracked up to be. Her room was dated and tiny, with a single divan bed pushed against the wall and a small wardrobe collecting dust in the corner. Her window offered a view of the main road, and I spent hours watching people pass by. It also doubled as a fire escape, and the two of us agreed that if I ever got caught by a cleaner I would run out of the room and down the ladders. We spent only four days there together before I got fed up, but while we lived in the B&B Amanda put me on the pill.

'I'll take you to the clinic,' she told me, explaining what I needed to do. 'It's easy.' Naively, I hadn't considered contraception before, but Amanda took charge, taking me along to the sexual health clinic where she signed the paperwork as my big sister.

'Samantha Spencer,' a nurse called out, and it took me a second to react.

'That's you,' Amanda hissed, having signed the forms with her last name. She pushed me to get up.

I liked that people thought we were sisters and I started to let Amanda pick out all the clothes I bought on our shopping trips. We wore matching velvet tracksuits and she helped me put my make-up on. I wanted to look exactly like her. Once a tomboy, strutting around in baggy jackets with David, I now felt pretty. I thought if I looked older then people would take me more seriously instead of treating me like a kid.

At the parties I would smoke a hashish pipe with some of the older men, or sit on the couch swigging vodka with Amanda, not stopping until I was paralytic.

'Three shots of vodka and a few drags fast gives you ten minutes of slut time,' Amanda informed me one night, waving her bottle of vodka in my face as I rolled myself a joint. To me, Amanda had so much more life experience than I did and I ate up every word she said. Heeding her instructions, I took three large gulps of vodka followed by a few drags of weed. After that, I started to feel dizzy and, chuckling to myself, I got up to dance.

An old man approached me, taking my hand. He must have been in his sixties. Getting drunk at the parties was so much easier than staying sober. I didn't care what happened to me; I had no feeling or emotion while I was wasted.

'If we're going to have sex,' I said to the man, as I stumbled from one foot to the other, 'we'd better do it quick.' Unable to even describe this man's face, I felt blank as he led me to a nearby bedroom and closed the door.

The more intoxicated I was, the less I worried about how awful the men were. Just don't think about it, I willed myself, trying to pretend that I was happy with what was happening. *I get something out of this.* Nonetheless, I'd still go home at the end of the night with tears in my eyes, playing the abuse over in my mind.

'Do you ever feel sick?' I asked Amanda one night. We were at a house we'd been to before but I didn't recognise anyone inside. The two of us had snuck outside the front door, smoking while we chatted.

'About what?' Amanda shrugged, not really interested in what I was trying to say.

'About the men,' I continued, glancing back to the house. 'They're disgusting.'

# PIMPED

'You'll get used to it, Sammy,' she replied, before heading back inside.

Once in the living room, she produced a small bag of white powder, saying, 'This might help.' She grinned, waving it under my nose. I watched her snort a line of coke before she carved a small strip for me. I leant my face over the table and did likewise. After a few minutes, the drug started to take effect. It was a nice feeling, like disco lights were flashing in my head. Suddenly I was completely numb and unaware of anything happening around me. I didn't care if anyone had sex with me. I doubt I'd have even known.

# 7.

# SAMANDA

The more parties we went to together, the more Amanda insisted we dress to look like one another.

'Come on, Sammy,' she argued with me one day. We were sat drinking at Spencer's house and Amanda was clutching a blunt earring stud in her hand. 'It won't hurt, I promise.'

'Yes it will,' I protested. Amanda had a diamond piercing above her top lip and she'd decided that I needed one too.

'It'll look right cool, though,' she persisted. 'We'll look the same.' I sighed. The thought of Amanda piercing my lip terrified me but I knew she wouldn't let it go until she got her way.

'Fine.' I gave up, exasperated. I took a gulp of my vodka and lemonade. 'Just make it quick.' With one hand she held my head in place and, with the other, shoved the earring through my lip. I screamed.

# PIMPED

'Fuck!' I exclaimed, cradling my face as my lip bled. 'That kills.' My eyes were watering as my lip throbbed but Amanda laughed, turning back to her drink.

'It'll be alright in a bit,' she remarked smugly. 'At least we match now.' That was her motto for everything we did: dyeing our hair, swapping our clothes, getting piercings. She also gifted me with a purple stiletto-shaped handbag, and I loved it. It was one of her hand-me-downs and I made sure to wear it whenever we went out. Everywhere we went, people thought we were sisters.

'Hey, Samanda,' a couple of the guys called over to us as we sat outside the markets. I grinned. Together, Amanda and I were a tribe.

One night, when I was still fourteen, Amanda took me to a house in Netherthorpe. The evening began normally: we drank at Spencer's flat before heading out to a party. I rolled a joint and lit it while we walked, as Amanda fixed her hair in her classic side ponytail. When we arrived at the house, I realised immediately that it was different to most of the other parties she had taken me to. The people inside were actually having fun. I listened to the music and laughter, excited. There was a mixture of ages, not just the standard group of old men lingering in the living room. Maybe she actually just wants to party with me, I thought, and I relaxed. Allowing myself to have a good time, I helped myself to the booze in the living room and turned to Amanda, beaming.

'This party has good vibes,' I mused, as the pair of us made our way through the crowd of dancers. The house itself was the familiar plain white-walled prison similar to every other place she had brought me to, but that didn't bother me. I was used to these surroundings by now.

I watched as she left the living room to speak to an Asian man in the hallway, before I turned away, continuing to pour myself a drink. The table in the room was a sea of alcohol and drugs, so I stole some weed, stashing it in my pocket for later. I was trying to navigate back out of the crowded room when out of nowhere someone pushed past me and I stumbled backwards into a shirtless man.

'Sorry,' I blurted out, steadying myself. The man was broad, Asian, and looked like he was in his twenties. Not saying anything, he looked me up and down. I was wearing a skirt and top that Amanda had picked out for me and my hair was in an identical ponytail to hers. Lowering his head, he whispered something in my ear, but the music was too loud for me to make out what he was saying.

'What?' I asked, and he repeated himself before I shook my head. 'Do you want to talk in the kitchen?' The man nodded and followed me to the back of the house.

'A hundred?' he asked bluntly once we were alone, and my heart sank. I knew exactly what he meant.

'Yeah, sure,' I replied, my voice faltering. 'A hundred pounds is fine.' I should have known better than to hope this was a real party.

Without a word he led me into a small bedroom. Like the living room, it was plain with white walls. There was a bed in the corner that looked dirty. I hope he doesn't want to have sex with me on that, I thought, revolted by the soiled sheets. I walked through the door and flicked the switch to turn the light off. I didn't need to see what was going to happen. The man shut the door behind him then wordlessly pulled down his pants and trousers, leaving them round his ankles. Without warning he grabbed me and bent me over, forcing himself inside me. It was so painful that I audibly yelped, clenching at the sharp pain.

What is this? I thought to myself. What am I doing? But I felt I deserved it because I hadn't confided in anyone about what Amanda was making me do. If only I'd told a social worker I wouldn't be being doing this right now, I berated myself. It's my fault. I half hoped that someone would walk in and catch us, witnessing for themselves this grown man having sex with a kid, but I knew that if anyone did catch us they'd just walk out again as if they hadn't seen a thing.

I started to tear up and was glad he couldn't see my face. He pushed the right side of my head into a pillow that was lying on the floor and I stared straight ahead. That wardrobe is missing its door, I thought, my eyes fixated on the empty closet in front of me. I wonder how that happened . . .

He wasn't treating me like a person and I dissociated, feeling like I was nothing. Afterwards, he pulled his pants up and left. Finally alone, I collapsed onto the floor, burying my face in the pillow. I sobbed. Maybe I'm not enjoying it because I'm not doing it right, I wondered. I couldn't understand how Amanda could happily do this. I crept out of the room and ran to the bathroom where I continued to cry in a heap on the floor. I hate this, I thought, using toilet roll to dry my eyes. My skin crawled across my body. *I feel vile.*

For days afterwards I couldn't get the events out of my head, replaying the rape over and over again in my mind. All I wanted was for someone to save me, or to tell me that what I was being made to do was wrong, but I was too embarrassed to mention it to anyone from social services and I knew my mum wouldn't listen.

Tired of the damp shed, I decided to spend a few nights at my children's home. A week after the party I sat alone in my bedroom and, in an act of desperation, dialled the helpline for the Samaritans. I waited anxiously, sat cross-legged on my bed, listening as it rang for a few beats before a woman answered. She asked how she could help and I suddenly froze, realising I hadn't thought through how I was going to tell her.

'Um,' I started, shifting uncomfortably, not wanting to go into detail. 'I want to talk to someone about something that happened.'

'Okay,' the woman encouraged me in a calm voice. 'Are you suicidal?'

'No, I just wanted to talk about something.' I cringed on hearing myself saying 'something' but I couldn't bring myself to explain the situation.

'Do you feel like you're going to kill yourself?' the woman repeated, and I began to wish I'd never made the call.

'No,' I told her. 'I . . .' I started to say before trailing off.

# PIMPED

I couldn't get my words out and I was starting to sweat with embarrassment.

'Okay,' the woman continued. Her soothing voice was starting to make me feel sick. 'What do you need to talk–' she began to say but I didn't let her finish, as I quickly put the phone down. *Well, that was of a waste of time.* I decided to never ring a helpline again. *They're just nosy anyway.* I felt like I had no one, nobody besides Amanda. She was the only person I could rely on and she had promised me that I'd get used to the parties, so I had no choice but to trust she was right.

The abandoned garage David, Chloe and I had shared had been discovered, so it was no longer an option to hide out there anymore but, while Chloe and I had stopped living together, the two of us became even closer as she started to occasionally tag along to parties with Amanda and me. I wasn't sure if Chloe knew what we were getting up to. She was usually so drunk, necking Lambrini until she was in hysterics, that I figured we were probably getting away with sneaking off to other rooms to have sex.

It was around this time that Amanda introduced me to Ian Foster. He was in his sixties and had a flat in the centre of Sheffield, by the shops. He was one of the men who lingered around the markets, along with Old Man John. John was an older man who sold the illegal counterfeit cigarettes, Jin Ling, and whenever I saw him I'd buy a pack. I knew Amanda had sex with Ian for money, but this had been the first time she had spoken about him to me.

# SAMANDA

Sometimes, when she had nowhere to go, Amanda would sleep at Ian's flat and, as the weeks went on, I joined her. Ian would sneak alcohol to us at the local pub, and for a while I enjoyed staying with him.

'Are you stealing that?' Ian asked me on a shopping trip to Primark one day. He'd clocked me slipping a dress into my bag.

'Obviously,' I remarked, sniggering at his question. *Why else would I be shopping?*

'Put everything you've taken into my basket,' Ian asserted, holding out his shopping basket towards me.

'Are you sure?' I was surprised and hoped he wasn't expecting anything in return, but Ian nodded and, with that, I handed over the clothes hidden in my bag. I liked the attention I got from Ian; he was almost like a father figure to me and he always treated me like I was a little girl. Ian bought me whatever I wanted and, when we went back to his, he left me alone, asking only Amanda for sex. This is great, I thought. I get to be here for free.

If Ian went to the corner shop, he'd always return with sweets for me. I didn't even have to ask.

'Alright, Samanda,' Ian said with a laugh, as he walked through the door. Amanda and I were chatting on his sofa. He didn't have a TV, which I frequently reminded him was a downside to staying at his.

'Hiya,' Amanda responded, as he tossed me a packet of chocolate-coated raisins. They were my favourite.

'Come on, then.' He gestured for Amanda to follow him

into his bedroom while I stayed on the couch. I waited in the living room, scoffing the chocolate while they had sex. Once she's slept with him, he'll let us drink, I thought, smiling to myself. What a good deal! I didn't sleep at Ian's every night but he was one of our options when we had nowhere else to go.

One day, after stopping over at my care home, I met up with Amanda by the bookies.

'Look,' she said, waving a bank card in my face. 'Look what I've got.'

'Did you steal it?' I asked, baffled by how she had got her hands on a card.

'Nope.' Amanda laughed. 'Ian gave me his credit card.' She had a massive grin plastered across her face.

'Oh my God,' I almost shouted with excitement. 'What shall we do?'

'Let's make the most of it,' Amanda replied, linking her arm with mine. 'We'll head to the shops first.' The rest of the day was spent joking around and spending Ian's money. It was great.

It was a few days later when I saw Ian again. I was short on booze and, being underage, there were limited places I could get my hands on any. I had watched Ian buy a bottle of vodka the week prior. I know he won't have finished it yet, I thought to myself, so I decided to pay him a visit.

'Have you still got that vodka?' I asked, as soon as he answered the door.

'Hello to you too, Sammy,' Ian joked, letting me in. I

invited myself into the living room, half-expecting to find Amanda sat on the sofa, but she wasn't there. It was rare that Ian and I were ever in the flat alone.

'I've still got some vodka,' he said, following me as I plonked myself down on the settee. 'Do you want some?'

'Definitely.' I smiled. I was still just fourteen but I was drinking so regularly that it was starting to take a lot to get me drunk. 'Can I have the bottle?' I asked, and Ian laughed.

'You want to keep the entire bottle?' he snapped back. 'And what do I get out of it?' At first his question caught me off guard. Ian had always given me whatever I wanted for free, so I didn't think this time would be any different.

'Um...' I hesitated, not sure what to say. 'I don't know.'

'I think you do know,' he replied, moving closer. I knew exactly what he wanted but I winced at the idea of having sex with him. I looked at his ugly face. There's no way this is happening, I thought, trying hopelessly to think up an excuse so I could leave. But as he got nearer I felt trapped. I was desperate for the vodka, and I already knew Ian, so I assumed it wouldn't be too bad.

'Right,' I agreed, reluctantly. 'Okay then.' I felt repulsed as Ian clambered on top of me. He was an old man, so I thought he would be gentle, and I hoped he'd be quick, but in reality Ian was very aggressive. I lay there staring at the ceiling while he hurt me. Then, out of the blue, Ian took hold of my neck with his hands, tightly gripping my throat. Horrified, I couldn't breathe. In terror I struggled as I tried to fight him off. He's strangling me, I thought, panicking.

# PIMPED

*I'm going to die!* Letting out a muffled scream, I wriggled myself free from his clutches.

'What the fuck are you doing?' I yelled, gasping for air. 'Stop it!' As I pushed him away, Ian tried to force himself back on top of me but I fought against him.

'What?' he eventually responded, giving up. Ian was much bigger than me but my adrenaline had kicked in and I felt stronger.

'You're a freak!' I shouted, trying to ignore the lump in my throat as I held back tears. I scrambled to my feet, biting my lip as I headed for the front door. The bottle of vodka was the last thing on my mind now. At first I was scared he'd chase after me, but I stormed out of his flat with such vengeance that I think he was too scared to follow. Even when I was having sex for money I knew my boundaries, and I wasn't ready to give up fighting so easily. They won't break me, I thought to myself. While the incident had frightened me, I still saw Ian from time to time when I went round to his with Amanda, but he never asked me for sex again.

I was still buying my cigarettes from Old Man John whenever I saw him in his spot by the markets, but one day Amanda made a shocking accusation to me.

'Sammy, Old Man John raped me.' We were sat near the markets, sharing a joint. I couldn't believe what I was hearing.

'That's awful,' I told her, taking a drag. 'Are you okay?'

'Of course I'm fine,' she quipped, laughing it off.

# SAMANDA

Sometimes I forgot how tough Amanda was. 'But I need to get revenge.'

She had decided that the best way to get back at John was to break into his house and steal all of his valuables. I didn't know whether to believe Amanda's story but, as always, I did what she asked and together we made our way to John's house. I waited at the front while Amanda walked round to make sure no one was home, not that she'd need to worry – he spent every waking minute selling his fake cigarettes in town.

'The coast is clear,' she announced as she returned, indicating for us to go inside. His living room window was slightly open and, being small, we managed to crawl through. We swiped whatever we could find: some jewellery, a bit of alcohol and even a little TV. We paraded our prizes around town, selling some stuff to the men at the markets. For me, it was a nice day out with my best friend. I was so used to Amanda's ways that I didn't think anything of it. Having sold off all of the stolen goods, we started to make our way home from the markets.

'Oi!' someone suddenly shouted from behind us, and the pair of us stopped dead in our tracks. I turned around to find Old Man John storming towards us.

'It wasn't us,' I blurted out in a panic, immediately regretting my words.

'Shut the fuck up, Sammy,' Amanda hissed, but John had already heard me. Without warning, he punched me square in the face and I staggered backwards in shock, steadying myself for a couple of seconds before he hit me again.

# PIMPED

'Shit,' I yelped, tasting blood in my mouth. John turned to face Amanda and I took my opportunity to run, fleeing up the town hall steps to watch from a safe distance. Amanda's the hardest girl I know, I thought, as I looked on. John doesn't know who he's messing with. But in reality Amanda was no match for him. Watching as he dragged her around by her hair, shaking and punching her, I found it almost comical.

'Get the fuck off me, you fucking fucker!' Amanda hollered, and I barked out a laugh. She can't fight for shit, I realised, losing a little bit of respect for the girl I'd so desperately looked up to. Eventually Amanda freed herself and ran for the hills. Seeing her flee from a fight, I couldn't help but question just how tough she really was.

That was the first fight Amanda had got me involved in but it wasn't the last. She was always getting into trouble with girls for sleeping with their boyfriends or slagging them off, and it often came down to me to sort them out. Old Man John saw the fight as payback for us stealing his stuff and he went back to selling us cigarettes as though nothing had happened, but it was only the beginning of the trouble that Amanda would get me involved in.

One early afternoon we were making our way into town. Standing at the city centre bus station, I lit a fag. We loitered around, smoking before planning to head to the markets, when we were stopped by a girl picking a fight with Amanda.

'Ew, here comes Jade,' Amanda said, lowering her voice

as a plump girl marched over to us. 'She's a right bitch.' I didn't know what Amanda had done but Jade was adamant about starting a fight with her.

The pair of them were older than me and it wasn't my fight so I stepped aside, letting them sort out their own argument. Out of nowhere, Jade started to throw punches at Amanda and I realised my friend wasn't handling the fight well. She's going to get battered by this girl, I thought, and, unsure of what to do, I worried Amanda was about to get seriously hurt. Thinking on my feet, I spotted a beer bottle abandoned on the side of the road. I picked it up and smashed the bottom on the kerb. Turning back to the girls, I made a beeline for Jade, my legs quivering as I walked. With the broken shards of glass in my hand, I pointed it at her until she stopped hitting Amanda.

'Woah!' Jade stepped back. I was only a little kid, skinny and weak, but standing up to Jade I looked fearless. She ran away, swearing as she went, leaving Amanda and me alone at the bus station.

'Well done.' Amanda patted me on the back. My legs were still shaking from nerves. I noticed I'd cut my arm from smashing the bottle and the marks were still visible weeks later. After that, Amanda always relied on me to back her up in fights and I resented her for it. All my scars were from sticking up for Amanda. Later on we'd laugh, chalking up the day's incidents to 'good times', but inside I was seething.

The cracks between us were beginning to form and I think Amanda could sense it. Remembering how cowardly she had been when confronted by Old Man John had made me realise how weak she actually was. She didn't scare me anymore and I was increasingly reluctant to do her any favours. I was fifteen now, I wasn't little, and at seventeen years old Amanda couldn't tell me what to do. The only hold she had over me was the parties. I relied on the free booze and money, so I'd join her on jobs at the houses, but we were hardly the unbreakable 'Samanda' that everyone still referred to us as.

I hadn't spoken to her for a few days when, completely skint, I agreed to go to a house with her one evening. We were in the kitchen, sitting drinking side by side at the table, when Amanda pulled out a cigarette. My shorts were riding up my bum so I shifted in my seat as Amanda lit her cig and took a drag. All of a sudden she took the cigarette in her hand and pressed it hard onto the top of my thigh.

'Ah!' I yelled, standing up to shake her off me. She cackled. 'You little shit,' I shouted, but that only made her laugh harder.

'Sorry,' she said, smirking, before taking another drag.

'Why would you do that?' I quizzed, rubbing the patch of skin she had burned. Amanda just shrugged.

'It was an accident,' she replied. I tried to brush it off, not wanting to cause a row, but afterwards I felt weird about the situation. *Why did she do that to me?* I knew it couldn't have been an accident. While we never spoke about it again, I couldn't help but feel it was punishment for not speaking to her.

# SAMANDA

Amanda was starting to annoy me and, whenever Chloe and I were together, we'd make fun of her behind her back.

'Ew, look at me,' I whined, as we sat in the Peace Gardens. I pushed my chest together. 'I'm Amanda and I've got massive tits.' We both burst into fits of giggles.

'Oh, you've been to Tenerife, have you?' Chloe mocked. 'I've been to Elevenerife.'

Amanda and I were growing more distant by the day. I enjoyed the money but I now hated hanging out with her. Not that Amanda really cared. When I rejected her calls, she'd hang out with her friend Olivia instead. Even though I was angry at Amanda, it still made me jealous to know Olivia was stealing my place. She started to take Olivia to parties instead of me. That's supposed to be my job, I ranted to myself.

I still couldn't bring myself to cut Amanda out completely. I made good money from the parties and I was completely hooked on the free drugs and alcohol. I was in too deep to turn back now.

Amanda had had her eyebrow pierced and, just like when she'd had her lip done, she demanded I did the same. I lay on the floor of some guy's living room as she pinned me down with a sewing needle. I was too intoxicated to remember if it hurt, but the next day my face was in agony.

Everything Amanda did with me, everything she called fun, caused me pain, but the final straw came down to a picture. I still had the same cheap blue wallet that I'd nicked from Poundland a couple of years earlier. It had butterflies dotted about the front and, on the inside, I had sellotaped a picture of my real dad. My mum had given it to me when I was a kid. I don't know why I kept it but having it with me felt comforting. I had never known my real father, but looking at the blurry photograph yellowing at the corners with age made me feel calm. We were at Spencer's when I noticed it was missing.

'Where's my wallet?' I asked, frantic that I'd left it lying around. Amanda shrugged, not looking at me.

'You can have one I've shoplifted,' she offered, but I shook my head.

'No, I need this one,' I replied, pulling out the sofa cushions in search of it. Amanda just sat there as I panicked, and I couldn't help but suspect she knew where it was. 'Have you taken it?' I accused her. I didn't put it past her to pickpocket me. 'You can keep the money in it, even keep the wallet for all I care. I just need the picture back.'

'It's just a picture' she retorted, rolling her eyes.

'Yeah, to you,' I countered. 'But not to me.'

Nothing I said would make Amanda confess to stealing the wallet, but she did hand me a new one that she'd taken from the shops a few days prior. I was devastated to have lost my dad's picture and I resigned myself to accept I would never see it again. Defeated, I sat in my bed at my children's home and opened up my new purse. A small photograph fell out and I picked it up to find Amanda had tucked a photo of herself into the sleeve. I stared at the picture, examining the blank expression on her face. It looked like a bus pass photo. My world already revolved around Amanda but in that instant a part of me realised that was because she had made sure of it. That photograph was the only thing I had owned of my real father and she took it away from me, just like she took away everything else.

# 8.

# MOVING AWAY

'Come on, Sammy, keep up,' Amanda shouted, barking orders at me from over the road. She and Olivia stood waiting for me at a bus stop as I crossed over. We'd spent most of the afternoon sitting in the Peace Gardens, drinking and smoking as we watched people pass by. I loved days like this; it was as close to being a normal teenager as we ever got, but Amanda's 'baccy man' sold his tobacco from the bus stop facing the gardens, so that was where we were headed.

'After this we'll go over to Debenhams and rob some jewellery,' Amanda told us as we walked, and I nodded obediently. Once we had met up with the baccy man I hung around waiting for Amanda to give us the go-ahead to leave.

'Such gorgeous girls,' the baccy man leered, noticing us

standing dutifully behind Amanda. I cringed. He was an old man and he looked homeless, always wearing the same green parka that was coated in a layer of filth and looked as though he'd had it on for years.

He moved his dirty face closer to Amanda's and I wrinkled my nose at the sight of his grey, scraggly beard touching her face. She giggled, passing him some change, and he handed her a bag of tobacco. I don't know how she can stand to flirt with him, I thought. He's disgusting. Amanda had been chatting away to him when, out of nowhere, he shoved his hand down her bra. I grimaced but Amanda burst out laughing.

'Ooh, I'm not yours anymore,' she cackled, moving his hand away from her. 'They are.' Amanda gestured towards me and Olivia, and I suddenly had a knot in my stomach. *What is that supposed to mean?* Terrified that this repulsive old git might take it as a signal to move closer to us, I tugged impatiently on Amanda's sleeve.

'Are we heading now?' I asked, the situation making me uneasy. 'I thought you wanted to shoplift.'

'Yeah,' she agreed. 'Let's go.' She waved goodbye and I breathed a sigh of relief, turning back to look at the baccy man as we left. He gave me a wink and I jumped, snapping my head back to face the road.

Shoplifting was something Amanda had down to a tee, perfected in her hardened years growing up in care.

'The trick is,' she said, holding a large handbag out in

front of me, 'to put tinfoil all over the inside so the sensors won't beep.'

'Really?' I asked in disbelief, unsure about her method. At first I was wary of her advice and, not wanting to get caught, I decided to give it a test run. Lining a small bag I'd taken from Poundland in aluminium foil, I wandered into Claire's Accessories. It was mine and Amanda's favourite shop and I knew everything had security tags. Cautiously placing a couple of pieces of jewellery into my bag, I rested it on the floor. Then, looking around to make sure no one had seen, I kicked the bag past the sensors. I held my breath, but when the alarm didn't go off I nearly squealed with excitement. Amanda was right. I grinned to myself. We can get away with taking anything!

After that, it felt like there was no stopping us. We lined our bags with a thick layer of tinfoil before filling them with clothes and jewellery from various shops. There were lockers at the local bus station, which, after putting a pound in the slot, we could use to stash our stolen goods while we ventured back out to lift more things.

'We've nailed this,' I laughed, taking our things out of the lockers at the end of the day. Amanda smiled at me.

'Too right,' she replied. 'Nothing will stop us.'

The shoplifting became a form of escape for me, something to focus on when I wasn't being dragged to parties. Between trips to the shops, Amanda and I still hung around the markets, often going to meet Old Man John. He took up his usual spot every single day from early in the morning until the stalls were closed. Another older man named Tony would often stand and chat to him but, unlike John, Tony was a nice man.

'Go home, petal,' Tony would tell me whenever we crossed paths. 'Get away from here.' I would smile and laugh, shaking my head at him.

'No chance,' I'd always reply, before running off to wherever Amanda was waiting. I didn't take Tony seriously. The market was mine and Amanda's playground – we were in charge, and there was no way I was leaving. Tony was only ever looking out for my best interests but John, on the other hand, was vile.

'You can come round to mine for tea if you like, Sammy,' he offered whenever I bought his cheap cigarettes. I hardly imagined John actually had any cooking in mind.

'No thanks,' I declined. 'I've already eaten.' I know what you're after, I noted to myself, grossed out by the creepy way he looked at me.

Old Man John was well known in the area, often going into shops to buy booze for the underage kids who hung around the markets. He always carried a flask with him, and sometimes he'd let us have a swig.

'Give us some fags, John,' Amanda and I would beg him whenever we were skint. 'We'll pay you back later.' John would roll his eyes but I knew he loved the attention he got from Amanda. She never seemed to care how ugly or old the men were; Amanda could flirt with anyone. Old Man John always ended up giving Amanda what she wanted.

It only took a few minutes of her pestering and he would back down.

'Fine,' he agreed, giving Amanda's bum a squeeze. 'Here you go.' And he would hand her a fistful of cigarettes.

While I enjoyed the influx of money from the parties, there were often days where Amanda hadn't paid me and I was completely broke. I needed money for cigs and food and, out of desperation, I'd have no choice but to ask for help. One day, hoping someone would let me borrow money, I spotted John in his usual spot and headed over to him.

'John, will you lend me twenty quid?' I asked, hesitating. 'Please.' John was leaning against a wall, puffing on a fag, and his eyes lit up.

'What do I get out of it?' He smirked. He looked thrilled that I'd asked him for help.

'I don't know,' I replied, hoping I wouldn't have to do him any favours.

'I need something in return,' John insisted, putting his arm around my shoulder. I shuddered.

'I'll meet you later,' I offered, and that was all the convincing he needed. John reached into his wallet and passed over a £20 note. As soon as the money was in my hands I fled, with no intention of meeting up with him later. *What an idiot. There's no way I'm meeting up with a creepy old man like him.* I laughed to myself, thinking I'd got away with it, but the next day John cornered me at the markets.

'You never met up with me yesterday,' he said, his face inches away from mine. 'Why's that?'

'I got arrested,' I lied, an excuse I'd heard Amanda use countless times before.

'Well,' John replied, looking me up and down, 'you owe me.' I felt sick. John was at least forty years older than me but I didn't have the money to pay him back. I looked around, hoping to spot someone who could save me from this situation, but there was no one familiar in sight.

'Right,' I agreed reluctantly, both of us understanding what that meant. Wordlessly, I followed him to an alleyway behind the market where he did what I had grown to expect from most men in my circle. I stayed silent the entire time, watching rainwater drip from a gutter above us. I was still just a child but I had been completely conditioned to accept rape as a form of payment. A few days later, John paid for me to get my ears pierced at Claire's Accessories.

'It's a reward for being a good girl,' he told me, and I rationalised what had happened earlier as a fair trade. As always, Amanda was with us both to sign the forms because I was still under sixteen. 'Samantha Spencer', she scribbled down without hesitation. We looked so similar that no one ever questioned it.

One day, the pair of us were spending the afternoon at the Moor, a strip of shops in the centre of Sheffield. We'd already nicked a few bits from Debenhams and, walking back to our locker with sleeves stuffed to the brim with stolen goods, we decided to cut through a nearby clothes shop. I held my breath as we stepped out of Debenhams but, glancing around, I couldn't see anyone following us.

We wandered through the doors of the next shop freely and I breathed a sigh of relief.

'Yes!' Amanda celebrated, as she marched ahead of me through the store. 'We did it.' The policy for the city centre lockers was that if you weren't back in an hour your items would be removed, so we needed to get there quickly. We both sprinted for the door but, as we neared the exit at the back of the shop, I felt a hand grab my shoulder. I spun around to find a tall security guard clutching the back of my shirt. *Crap*. I panicked and turned back to see Amanda had made a break for it. I watched her as she ran through the store, only to be caught by more security waiting for her at the entrance. The pair of us were then taken into a back room where we were left alone while the security phoned the police.

'We've lost the stuff in the lockers,' I grumbled once everyone was out of sight, but Amanda wasn't paying attention; instead she stared blankly ahead.

'You need to take the rap for this,' she blurted out after a few minutes of silence. 'I can't get the blame for it.'

'What?' I replied, shocked by what she was asking of me. *Why am I always the one doing her favours?* I was unsure as to whether she would ever do the same for me.

'You're still under sixteen,' she explained. 'But for me, with my record, I'll go to prison.' I felt racked with guilt. On the one hand, I didn't want to take the sole blame for what we'd done together but, on the other, I didn't think I could let Amanda go to prison for it if I could help her.

'What will happen to me, though?' I asked, scared they'd send me down anyway.

'You'll be fine,' she reassured me. 'You're still underage, so they'll probably let you off. Just make sure you say it was all your fault.' I gulped, not knowing how to respond.

Once the police arrived they took us to the nearest station, where Amanda and I were split up. Alone in a room with a police officer, I lied through my teeth to make sure Amanda was let off the hook.

'Are you sure it was your idea?' the officer quizzed, giving me a chance to change my mind. 'You don't want to make a different statement?' I shook my head, determined to stand by my best friend.

'I did it,' I repeated, wanting him to believe the lie. 'Amanda is innocent in this.' I still held onto the blind hope that Amanda was right when she'd told me everything would be fine, but it wasn't.

'I think we're going to have to move you out of Sheffield,' one social worker informed me in a later meeting. 'Given the circumstances, it's important for you to be away from bad influences.'

'What?' I replied in horror. 'You can't send me away.' I had been given a court date to attend in a few months' time, and while I waited for it social services wanted me as far away from Amanda as possible. Deep down I knew separating us was probably for the best, but by this point I couldn't imagine being without her.

'We've found a children's home in Chesterfield that

would be more suitable for you,' the social worker continued, ignoring my protests. 'It's semi-independent and we really think you would benefit from the change in environment.'

The thought of leaving everyone behind was devastating but I didn't have a choice. Chesterfield was about fourteen miles away from Sheffield and, while it wouldn't be impossible for me to sneak back into the city if I needed to, it was still far enough that I wouldn't be constantly under Amanda's watchful eye. With no other option I was sent home, where I reluctantly packed my bags. It's not fair, I thought to myself, stuffing my clothes into plastic bags.

The social worker sent to escort me knocked on my door. 'Do you need any help? Or are you ready to go?' I looked around my bedroom. I barely spent any time at the children's home as it was and there wasn't much in the room I would miss.

'I'm ready,' I called back and, after taking one last look around, I made my way downstairs. The car was waiting outside. I slid into the back seat, the internal rage occupying my mind. I guess this is the thanks I get for covering for Amanda, I thought bitterly, now regretting the lie I'd told to save her arrest. The thirty minutes it took to drive to Chesterfield were quiet and I sat staring out of the window, each mile on the motorway dragging me further away from everything that was familiar.

'Here we are.' The social worker broke the silence and I realised we were pulling up outside a house. I was shown to my new bedroom. It's just another boring room, I thought, and, unimpressed, sat down on the bed.

'What do you think?' she asked me and I shrugged.

'All kids' homes look the same,' I snapped bluntly. 'So it doesn't really matter.'

'I think you'll really like it here,' she replied, unfazed by my comments. 'You'll soon get your bearings,' she added, before leaving me alone to unpack my things. I wasn't on my own for long as, a few minutes later, a teenage boy poked his head around the door.

'Hi,' he chirped, giving me a wide grin. 'I'm James.'

'Oh hi,' I answered, caught off guard. James was around the same age as me and the pair of us soon became good friends, hanging out at the children's home together. James owned a few video games that he kept in his room and, letting me sit with him one day, he handed me a controller.

'Hit the X button to shoot,' he instructed, and I took the controller from him. The pair of us spent the afternoon laughing and playing games. All I wanted was to forget my past but, unable to cut ties completely, I would still occasionally sneak back to Sheffield when I was desperate for money. The trips occurred less and less, though, and I soon started to see the separation from Amanda as a welcome break. Making friends with James helped me to settle into my new life in Chesterfield and the incentive to see Amanda dwindled.

One particular day, I was making my way back home from the corner shop when I noticed a teenage boy walking the other way. He was tall with a slim build, wearing no top as he strode by me. He didn't acknowledge or even look at me but I fancied him immediately. I've not seen him before, I thought, as I headed home. I tried to shake the boy from my mind, but for several days after that I'd see him on the street from my bedroom window, wandering to a house across the road.

'There he is!' I pointed the boy out to James and he laughed.

'Oh, that's Blaine,' he told me, moving away from the windowsill.

'Who's Blaine?' I asked, curious to find out who the mystery boy was.

'Just some kid I know.' James paused for a second. 'Actually, I'm going round to his house tomorrow if you want to come along.' I beamed. I didn't know anyone in Chesterfield yet and I needed to make friends.

'Sure, why not,' I agreed. I tried to sound cool but I was secretly excited to finally be meeting Blaine.

The next morning, James and I ventured over the road, knocking on the door I'd seen Blaine emerge from several times. When he answered, my stomach did flips.

'Oh hey,' Blaine said, smiling. 'Come on in, I'll just be a second.' He let us into the hallway. He was still in his pyjamas, so as he ran upstairs to get changed, James and I waited by the front door.

'He's well fit,' I whispered to James, who rolled his eyes.

'Shut up,' he replied, laughing at me. After a couple of

minutes, Blaine reappeared at the stairs and gestured for us to come up. The three of us spent the day watching films and playing video games together. Laughing and joking with Blaine and James made me feel like a normal fifteen-year-old for once; there was no looming party I had to attend, and no Amanda forcing me to meet strange men. Life was great. A few hours later, James started getting ready to leave.

'Come on,' he said, shrugging his jacket over his shoulders. 'We're going, Sam.' But I had been having so much fun that I wasn't ready to go yet. I wanted to stay.

'It's alright,' I replied, sticking to my cross-legged spot on the floor. 'I'll catch you later.'

James said his goodbyes before heading back to the children's home but I stayed behind to watch another film with Blaine. We got on so well that we shared a quick kiss that day and, afterwards, Blaine started texting me nonstop. We met up almost every day after that, and for the first time in my life I felt like a proper teenager. I was fifteen and Blaine was eighteen, but he made me feel that childlike innocence and excitement I'd long forgotten. It was as though I had got my childhood back. He never expected sex from me, and it was months before anything sexual happened between us. Instead, we would just have a laugh together, play-fighting or having silly dance-offs. We were always immature around each other, and spending time with Blaine was a much-needed distraction and antidote from the pressures of being friends with Amanda.

His mum would cook tea for me whenever I went

round, and on the weekends I joined in the family BBQs. It wasn't long before Blaine and I were in a relationship and, once that was the case, Amanda and I were no more. I couldn't bear the thought of cheating on him so I decided to cut her out, not wanting to go on jobs for her anymore. I desperately wanted to make it work with Blaine and I knew Amanda would try to sabotage it if she knew I was happy without her.

I changed my phone number and, with her out of my life, I began to see glimpses of a future where I could be happy. Being with Blaine made me see what a normal life could be like and I even started dreaming of the possibility of having kids and getting married.

'Are you gonna take your shoes off?' Blaine asked me one afternoon and I laughed, kicking my trainers to the floor. Like most days, I was sat on the end of his bed watching a film. I had my favourite velvet tracksuit on and, as always, my hair was tied up to one side. We started to kiss and, sensing where it was leading, I panicked.

'I'm a virgin,' I blurted out, immediately feeling guilty for the lie. I was terrified that if Blaine knew the truth he would judge me for my past or, even worse, not want to be with me anymore. All I wanted was to pretend that all that abuse had never happened. Blaine wasn't fazed by my announcement and the first time we had sex really did feel like I was losing my virginity. I wasn't drunk or coerced; this was the first time it was truly my choice. The way I see it is that I *did* lose my virginity to him.

# PIMPED

Sleeping with Blaine, I discovered the difference between having a choice and being forced into sex, and it made me realise that all of the other times with older men was rape. It was as though a light bulb had suddenly clicked on in my head. I resigned myself to keeping it a secret forever. Blaine is never going to find out the truth because I'm never going to tell him, I told myself but, even so, the telltale signs were there. When we had sex, I'd have flashbacks to incidents in the past and Blaine would be confused when I made him stop. He could sense something wasn't right, so I eventually knew I needed to give him an explanation.

'I was raped,' I stated out of the blue, breaking down in tears. I didn't go into detail and Blaine didn't ask me questions; he just quietly understood. Telling him felt like a relief. I had been hiding such a big part of my life, and even though he didn't know the extent of what had happened he knew enough to understand why I acted the way I did. After that, he was even gentler with me and everything felt right in the world.

I avoided going back to Sheffield as much as I could, only making the odd trip here and there to visit my mum and siblings. Even when I did go back, I was careful not to bump into anyone I knew and I never stayed for long.

On the last trip I made, before I was due to appear in court, I stumbled upon Amanda and Olivia in the city centre. I had been shopping at the Moor and was heading back to my mum's house when I heard someone call out my name.

'Oi, Sammy!' Amanda shouted, and I turned, giving her a forced smile.

# MOVING AWAY

'Hey,' I replied, noticing Amanda had a set of bright pink plastic hair extensions clipped onto her scalp. They looked so cheap. 'How's it going?'

'Brill, we've not seen you in ages.' She swished her hair around. 'Have you seen my extensions?'

'Yeah, they look great,' I answered, unable to hide the sarcastic tone in my voice. I was so over being friends with her by now. I glanced at Olivia; her skin was so pale that she looked ill.

'We can rob some extensions for you too, Sammy,' Olivia offered, noticing that I was staring right at her.

'No, that's alright.' I hesitated. Part of me wanted to ask Olivia if she was okay but I was cautious of saying anything in front of Amanda. 'I'll see you both soon,' I added awkwardly, unsure of how to make my exit. She's really out of my life for good, I thought, as I walked away, willing the painful saga of Amanda to be over.

Once back in Chesterfield, I decided not to say anything to Blaine about my upcoming court appearance. I was far too embarrassed to tell him, so I battled with the dilemma by myself. *There's no point. It won't do any good.*

It was April 2009 when I stood before Sheffield Magistrates Court. I had pleaded guilty in the hope that it may lean in my favour but, alone in the dock, my heart raced as the magistrate read over my case. This will be fine, I told myself, imagining going home that evening to Blaine. What's the worst that can happen? I told myself. But the more I listened to my case being read out the more I started to panic.

# PIMPED

'Samantha Owens,' the magistrates eventually called, and I looked up, tapping my foot nervously against the carpeted floor. 'I'm sentencing you to twenty-eight days at a young offenders institute,' he began to tell me, but the rest was a blur. No! I screamed internally, this is not happening. I squeezed my eyes shut, unable to comprehend what I was hearing.

I was taken away from the dock and, as I sat in the back of a car, being driven to Wakefield, I wondered what Blaine would think. Is he going to find out? I pondered to myself. Or will he think I've just abandoned him? I sat in silence as we drove towards HMP New Hall. The picture-perfect idea in my head of a dreamy future with Blaine was starting to fade.

# 9.

# LOCKED UP

**H**MP New Hall was a women's prison in Wakefield, about twenty-six miles north of Sheffield. Upon arrival, I was taken to the young offenders unit. A warden handed me paperwork detailing why I was there and, as I was led inside, my mind raced, picturing the worst – cramped cells and prison fights. I was so nervous that it felt like my heart was going to burst out of my chest but, when the warden showed me to my room, I breathed a slight sigh of relief. I had the space to myself and, while the room was basic, it felt safe.

A metal-framed bed stood in the corner supporting a plastic mattress, and beside the bed was a plastic desk and chair. There was a small TV on top of the desk and on one of the plain white walls hung a floral canvas. This isn't too awful, I thought, and started to calm down. I even had my own toilet and shower attached to my room. I thought, I can survive twenty-eight days in here.

The warden handed me a grey tracksuit but, as long as my clothes were modest, I was allowed to wear what I wanted. That night I lay on my bed wondering if Blaine was sat at home trying to ring me. I'm doing a good thing, I convinced myself, attempting to shake off the sense of guilt settling in my stomach. *At least I'm in a juvenile unit. If I hadn't taken the blame, Amanda would be in actual prison right now.* Despite everything she had put me through, I still had a sense of loyalty to Amanda ingrained in my mind. I'm here to help Amanda, I resolved and, with that, I managed to get some sleep.

At 7 a.m., an alarm blared through speakers around the prison to wake us up. In a daze, I dragged myself out of bed, squinting sleepily as I threw on a shirt and tracksuit bottoms. I hurried to get ready so I could stand outside my door for roll call. I peered down the hall at the other girls lining up as a warden walked up and down, counting us all. Act hard, I told myself, putting on the toughest look I could muster, but deep down I felt like a rabbit caught in headlights. A couple of the other girls glanced over at me before looking away and, nervous, I focused my gaze straight ahead until the warden was finished. After roll call, we were all let into the canteen for breakfast. I shuffled along, following the crowd into the hall before joining the growing queue for food.

'What are you having?' the woman asked once I'd reached

the front of the line. She looked like a prisoner from the adult unit.

'Um. . .' I looked around at the options. 'Eggs, beans and toast please.' The woman nodded, bending down to the food laid out in front of her, then scooping it onto my tray.

I thanked her and meekly made my way to a seat, willing myself to keep my head up in front of the other prisoners.

'What are you in for?' one girl asked right away, moving her chair to my table so she could sit beside me.

'Shoplifting,' I answered, not looking up from my plate.

'Let me see your deps, then,' she replied, extending her hand towards me.

'My what?' I asked, looking up at her. I didn't understand what she meant.

'Your deps,' she repeated. Her hand was still stretched out expectantly. 'For your sentence.'

'Oh.' I realised she meant the paperwork the warden had given me. I reached into my pocket and pulled out the folded-up paper. 'Here,' I said, handing it over. One glance at my crime description seemed to satisfy her; she passed it back, got up and left. That was weird, I thought, but that day nearly everyone who spoke to me wanted to know why I was there and I spent all morning passing around my paperwork to various girls.

After breakfast we were sent to another part of the building for compulsory education. Even though we had to attend, we were given £10 a week for sitting in on classes. At first that didn't sound like a lot, but it went a long way in prison and the first thing I spent my tenner on was nice shampoo and toiletries. Throughout the day I couldn't help but notice how some of the other young offenders were trying to be intimidating. It was as if they were testing me.

'Only shoplifting?' one girl sniggered, holding up my papers. 'I'm in here because of way worse things.' She chucked the paper back at me, laughing along with a couple of other girls. I took a deep breath. I had learnt quickly that I had to be intimidating back if I wanted to survive the next four weeks. If I don't respond then I'll look weak, I thought, as the girl got up to walk away. I'll be the first target to be terrorised if I don't act tough.

'Yeah,' I replied, getting her attention. 'I'm only in for shoplifting because I didn't get caught for the other stuff.' I winced, cringing inside as I heard myself speak. But standing up earned me a little respect and it wasn't long before I started to blend in with the rest of the girls. The prison served dinner at 5 p.m. and after that it was shower time before we had to be back in our rooms. We were allocated one phone call in the evening, which I always used to ring my siblings.

'Hiya Mum,' I said, as she answered the phone. 'Put the kids on.' I waited while there was a couple of seconds of silence.

'Sammy!' I heard a young voice shout before a chorus of noise and laughter erupted from my three youngest siblings, Jordane, Brandon and Chelsea. Mum had recently been getting more visiting time with them and the youngest ones were living with her again. I smiled, listening to their innocent voices chatter away down the phone.

Once I'd used up my call for the night, I was left to spend the rest of the evening back in my room. I had a small cork board above my desk and I occupied myself colouring in pictures of Tatty Teddy drawings to pin up. The juvenile unit had a strict no smoking policy and, for the first time in two years, I was completely sober. Not only was I clean of cigarettes but I was free from the haze of weed and alcohol too. I started to see everything clearly again but I began to miss things I had taken for granted before, whether it was mundane acts like walking to the shop or even straightening my hair. I missed having control over my own life and I desperately missed spending time with my siblings.

I had been there a few days when, during a period of free time we'd been given in between lessons, I sat at a table with a group of girls. I was chatting to someone when suddenly I heard what sounded like a familiar voice.

'You've got a broad Sheffield accent, haven't you?' I exclaimed to the girl next to me, surprised and excited to recognise her voice.

'Yeah,' the girl replied. 'I'm from Sheffield.' She was petite and pretty with long, wavy blonde hair.

'Me too.' I beamed and we immediately bonded over our hometown.

'Do you ever hang out at the Peace Gardens?' she asked me.

'Yeah, all the time.' I grinned. 'And the markets.' After just a few days in prison, home was already starting to feel like a distant memory and it was comforting to hear her talk about places I knew. I discovered her name was Bunny and we knew a lot of the same people.

'Do you know David Dable?' I asked after a few minutes, excited to know if she had heard of my brother.

'Yeah, I've slept with him,' Bunny told me.

'Ew, that's gross, he's my brother!' I cried out, pulling a face. 'I wish you hadn't told me that.' Bunny laughed and we continued reeling through a list of people we might know.

'Do you know Amanda?' Bunny eventually mentioned and, hearing that name, of course my ears pricked up.

'Amanda who?' I quizzed her. *Surely she can't mean the same Amanda.*

'Amanda Spencer.' My jaw dropped to the floor.

'As if you know Amanda Spencer!' I burst out, almost yelling with enthusiasm. 'She's my best friend.'

'Really?' She seemed surprised. 'Do you know what she does?'

'What she does?' I repeated. I was confused and her question had taken me by surprise. 'She doesn't work.'

'No, I used to work for her,' Bunny continued.

'What do you mean?' I queried. 'I don't know what you're on about.' Bunny looked around the room before pulling me to one side.

'She sells vulnerable girls for money,' she hissed, lowering her voice. 'She targets them.' My stomach dropped.

'What?' I couldn't seem to stop shaking my head, unable to accept what Bunny was telling me. 'I don't know what you mean.'

'She grooms girls so she can sell them to . . . like . . .' Bunny paused: 'sex rings'. I felt a pang of pain in my stomach as Bunny's words started to feel uncomfortably familiar. 'Didn't you know?' she added, and I shook my head.

'I know she's a prostitute,' I replied, trying to clarify what she was getting at. 'She sells sex for money but I've done that with her too.'

'No,' Bunny insisted. 'She sells girls on for money. She takes advantage of them.' I couldn't believe what I was hearing. Amanda had always intimidated me but I saw us as equals – we were friends. I tried to shake the seed of doubt growing in my mind but my thoughts raced to all the times Amanda had sent me off to parties, instructing me as to which houses were expecting me. All the times Amanda had paid me afterwards, often not giving me as much as I knew the men had paid her.

'But Amanda and I are in the same boat,' I slowly started to say. 'She wouldn't do something like that.' I wasn't sure if even I believed my own words as Bunny shrugged.

'Well, she's done it to me before,' she admitted. I started to ask about which parties Bunny had been to but we were interrupted by a warden.

'Time for roll call,' he announced, and we were all sent back to stand by our rooms to be counted. As I waited for the roll call to end, I stared at Bunny down the corridor. She was standing in her spot outside her room a few doors away. Amanda sells girls? I battled internally, confused by what that meant. Is Bunny telling me the truth? Bunny looked briefly back at me before we were sent into our rooms. She's a lying bitch, I decided, in total denial of reality.

My room was just big enough to walk around in and I paced back and forth, analysing our previous conversation. Why is she stirring up rumours about Amanda? I asked myself, but at the same time the sinking feeling in the pit of my stomach wouldn't go away, and I couldn't help but think Bunny knew too much about Amanda for it to be a lie. I felt compelled to justify Amanda's actions – that I wanted to go back out there and stand up for her like a best friend should – but the more I thought it over, the more stupid I felt for ever being friends with her in the first place. One thing kept playing on my mind: *did Amanda sell me to all those men?* It was as if a screen had shattered in my thoughts and, in the sober light of day, I could finally see Amanda clearly. Did she specifically target me so she could take advantage? I thought back to all the times I'd reluctantly agreed to sleep with those vile men. I had been coerced.

I didn't speak to Bunny about Amanda again after that. The overwhelming sense of dread and guilt I got whenever I thought about it was almost too much to bear. Even though I had never met Bunny before, I felt somewhat responsible for what Amanda had done to her. Does Bunny think I'm also to blame? I agonised. After all, I am Amanda's best friend. I wanted to cry at the notion of it and I wondered how many other girls Amanda had taken advantage of.

From the one conversation I'd had with Bunny, I knew everything I needed to know but, instead of bringing it up, I kept my head down, focusing on my release date. I still felt somewhat in denial about Amanda, but the closer I got to getting out of prison the more I started to admit to myself what she'd done. *Did Amanda prepare me to be pimped out?* I felt violated and it hurt to think about it. In a way, I saw her as being worse than the men who'd abused me; she had led me there and had profited from my pain. Everything about our friendship had been a lie.

My sixteenth birthday came and went in prison without much recognition and, as much as I tried to forget the past, I couldn't get Amanda out of my mind. The more I thought about her, the angrier I became. She used me, I raged to myself, furious that she had been getting away with this. I came to a decision: *I need to tell someone.*

The day before I was due to be released, I made my way to the counselling offices within the prison. We were allowed to go there whenever we needed to talk about issues. We had all been allocated a youth officer upon arrival, and mine was a middle-aged woman named Claire. I felt compelled to go to her office. I stood outside her door, holding my breath before giving a small knock.

'Come in,' Claire called, and I cautiously opened the door, giving her a small nod as I took a seat at her desk. 'How are you, Samantha?' she asked, smiling at me. Claire was always nice to me and I thought I could confide in her about almost anything, but now that I was actually sat in front of her with something important to say, I felt sick.

'I'm alright,' I lied, settling into my chair. I shifted around uncomfortably, unsure what else to say.

'So . . .' Claire filled the silence, watching me fidget nervously. 'What can I help with?' The situation with Amanda had been on my mind and bothering me all hours of the day, but suddenly I couldn't speak. I counted myself down, plucking up the courage to say something. *Three, two, one . . . go.* But not so much as a word came out of my mouth. Instead, I sat rooted to the spot, my cheeks flushing red with embarrassment.

'Take your time,' Claire comforted me. 'What do you want to talk about?'

'I was raped,' I blurted out. A huge rush of relief washed over me, and once I'd spoken it was like I couldn't stop. 'Amanda Spencer is the girl who made me do it. She sold me to men.' My cheeks burned even harder as Claire looked back at me in shock. 'And it started when I was thirteen.' Embarrassed, I buried my head in my hands as Claire calmly reassured me.

'Thank you for confiding in me, Samantha,' she began, explaining that she would report what I'd told her to the police. I relaxed, telling her all about the parties and the shopping sprees. An adult was finally listening. I smiled, relieved to not be keeping this to myself anymore. I left Claire's office, shut the door behind me and froze, immediately regretting everything I'd just said. Have I gone mad? I thought, wishing I could run back into her office and take everything back. *Amanda will kill me if she finds out what I've done.* I knew I was being released the following day and I was petrified of what might happen next.

I chewed my lip as I headed back to my room, going over the possible scenarios. Claire is just another screw, I told myself. She doesn't really care about me. Nothing will come of it. She seemed concerned but I doubted anyone would take me seriously.

The next morning, at 8 a.m. on the dot, I was escorted out of the prison. Setting foot outside of those doors, I took in my surroundings, appreciating the smell of grass from the lawn out the front. Freedom. The prison had paid for a taxi, which was waiting to take me to the train station and, from there, I had a travel pass to get me home. I thought about Blaine and the future I had so desperately hoped for, but I was sixteen years old now and no longer considered a care kid, so I was sent to live in a flat in Sheffield. Back to square one.

# 10.

# RELEASED

Sitting in the taxi on the way to the station, I rolled the window down, letting the fresh morning air hit my face. I can't believe it's over, I thought, mentally congratulating myself on surviving life as a young offender, relieved to be on the other side. I can't let that happen again.

Once we arrived at the station, I pulled my bag out of the boot and waved thanks to the driver. Upon leaving the prison, a warden had handed me a carrier bag containing all of my things and I clutched it with both hands as I wandered through the ticket barriers and boarded my train. Easing myself into the seat, I felt like a weight had been lifted off my shoulders. I just want life to be normal, I thought, wondering if Blaine had forgotten about me by now.

Within an hour I'd arrived back in Sheffield and it was as if I'd never left. I wandered through the city centre. Nothing has changed, I mused. It was a bright June morning and the streets was already filling up with people heading to work. I'm starving, I thought, realising I hadn't eaten anything yet that day. I made my way to a local bakery and came away with a bacon butty. I jumped on the bus with my breakfast and headed to my new home. The flat I had been allocated was in a high-rise block on Brightmore Drive. It was situated in Netherthorpe, just a stone's throw from many of the parties I'd been to with Amanda. Walking past the familiar houses, I shuddered. *I don't ever want to go back to that.* My flat was small and basic, with damp growing in the corners, but it was my home now and I was determined to make it nice. I picked up bits and bobs from Poundland and, as I placed my new candles down on the coffee table, I cheered up. *Living here won't be so bad.*

As much as I wanted to, I still couldn't forget what Bunny had told me. Amanda had used me and I needed to confront her about what she'd done, so the next day I went in search of her around town. I walked past the Peace Gardens, scanning the groups of teenagers smoking together, but there was no sign of Amanda. I headed for the shops, cutting through the markets, and bumped into Old Man John.

'Hey, have you seen Amanda today?' I asked, as I watched him light a fag.

'Nope, sorry, I've not seen her all day,' he replied, before gesturing towards his cigarette. 'But do you want to buy any?'

'No thanks,' I declined. I had cleaned up my act in prison and I was trying to keep my resolve not to fall back into bad habits. Giving up on finding Amanda, I headed home but returned the next day to continue my search. *Where the hell is she?* I wondered, searching high and low throughout the city centre. I wandered up and down the Moor but there was no sign of her. When the markets started to close, I realised I wasn't going to have any luck and decided to call it a night.

On the way home I sat at the back of the bus staring out of the window. *She's getting away with hurting young girls,* I told myself, and I felt stupid for letting her into my life. That night I vowed to go back into the centre every day until I found her, and I didn't have to wait long. On the third day of searching I spotted her loitering outside the bookies. Watching her from a distance, I could see her laughing smugly, flirting with the six men who surrounded her. I recognised the baccy man from the Peace Gardens; he leered over her, grabbing at her as she laughed. I rolled my eyes. *How embarrassing,* I thought, seeing her flounce around in her massive hoops.

She wore a blue body warmer with a crop top underneath and her hair was tied to the side, as usual. I was tempted to walk away and forget about her. I just wanted to move on with life and any interaction with Amanda only ever held me back. I hesitated, debating whether I should leave until, suddenly, I spotted her chatting to a couple of young girls. *This isn't happening.* I stood in shock, watching her brag as the girls listened to her. I was livid. A blind anger washed over me and, without a second thought, I marched over. She noticed I was making a beeline for her.

'What's up?' she asked, as soon as I was in earshot. I glared at her, unable to hide the rage on my face.

'You fucking know what's up with me,' I blurted out. My anger had built up so quickly that I felt my cheeks burn. 'I've just been inside and someone's told me everything.' Amanda let out a cackle, looking back to her crowd as they sniggered along with her.

'Have you gone mad?' She flailed her arms dramatically, as if to ridicule me. 'Go home, Sammy,' she said, in her patronising voice.

'No.' I wasn't about to let her shut me up now. Once I'd started talking I couldn't stop. 'I know what you've done.'

'I haven't done anything.' Amanda smirked, crossing her arms over her chest. 'What are you on about?'

'I'm on about you,' I said hesitantly, my eyes starting to prick with tears. I took a deep breath. 'You, selling girls.' Her face immediately dropped.

'You're lying, you're lying,' she protested, but her voice had lowered.

'No, I'm not,' I shouted back, purposely raising my own voice. 'I know what you've been doing to vulnerable girls.'

Amanda hushed me, attempting to move us both away from the group of people near us. Anyone in the centre who knew Amanda was aware she slept around but not everyone knew it was for money; we didn't exactly boast about selling ourselves for sex. Amanda tried to guide me into the nearby alleyway but I wouldn't budge.

'Come on,' she whispered, tugging on my arm to get me

to move. I knew she didn't want anyone to hear what I had to say so I stood my ground, refusing to leave the spot.

'You can't tell me what to do,' I argued, pushing her away from me. 'I know you've groomed girls.'

'You're lying,' Amanda spat back, looking to the group around her to back her up. 'Knock her out,' she ordered, but no one moved. Instead, her crowd just watched, giggling between themselves at the prospect of a fight. She turned back to look me in the eye as I stared at her. In that moment I truly loathed Amanda. *How dare she deny what she's done!*

I felt the anger get the better of me and, in a haze of blind hatred, I punched her square in the face. My fist hit her cheekbone with a crack and, at first, the pair of us both looked at each other in shock that I'd just hit her. She staggered backwards before regaining her balance. In silence, she peered back once again for someone to stick up for her but nobody did – that had always been my job. She didn't try to hit me back. Instead she just stood there, frozen, with her mouth wide open. Everyone used to gossip about how hard Amanda was, and thinking back to all the times she had intimidated me almost made me laugh. She didn't say a word as she stared at me. It was as if she couldn't believe I'd dared to stand up to her at last. I'm going to cry, I thought, and panicked as the adrenaline was starting to wear off. I turned on my heels and stormed off to the bus station. I tried my best to walk away with swagger, not wanting anyone to know I was upset. For the duration of my walk to the station, I couldn't help but glance over my shoulder repeatedly, half-expecting Amanda to come screaming down the street, but she didn't. No one followed me.

Once I was on the bus, I took a long breath. Suddenly all of the anger I had held towards Amanda turned into hurt. I've just lost my best friend, I realised, and I teared up. I couldn't understand how our entire friendship had been a lie. We were Samanda. Rubbing my grazed knuckles, I fought back tears the whole way home.

After that, I didn't see Amanda for weeks and I focused my attention on rebuilding my life. Blaine and I got back in touch. We still cared about each other, and I couldn't imagine a future without him, but my life was too chaotic for us to make our relationship work. I didn't trust anyone and our fights often led to me believing he would abandon me. Even still, Blaine and I remained friends and sometimes he would even come from Chesterfield to visit me in my high-rise flat.

'Are you doing alright?' he asked me one day, noticing the lack of food in my fridge.

'Yeah, I'm fine,' I lied. I was too embarrassed to admit to him that I was struggling to make ends meet. I was desperately trying to build a normal life for myself away from Amanda, but the poorer I was the harder it was becoming to stay away from her.

'You know if you're stuck I'll help you,' Blaine offered. I smiled at him. Blaine was the only person who really cared about me.

'Thanks,' I replied, not giving away how much I needed

his help. 'But I'll be okay. I always am.' I didn't want Blaine to have to bail me out of trouble every time I sank into a slump and I was too proud to admit that I needed him, but things only got worse. I desperately tried to get a job but, with my record, no one would hire me. Eventually I knew I was going to have to ask someone for help. Mum lived just one street away from me at the time and she was my last resort.

'Hiya,' I said, grinning as she opened the door. We were the closest we had ever been and I visited her most days.

'Hey, Sam,' she answered, stepping to the side. 'Come on in.' I took a seat in her living room. Mum had been doing a lot better since Joe had been out of her life and the youngest children were living with her again.

'The kids will be sorry they missed you,' she said, handing me a cup of tea before plonking herself down next to me. 'They're at school.'

'Aw, I'll come to see them soon,' I replied. I loved spending time with my siblings. Mum and I chatted for a while, catching up on each other's lives.

'How are you, then?' she asked, taking a sip from her mug. I didn't know how to broach the subject of money and I felt embarrassed having to ask.

'Mum,' I started to say, feeling myself heat up with apprehension. I hated to admit things had got to this point. 'I'm really struggling actually.'

'What's the matter?' she queried. Even though my mum and I hadn't always had the best relationship, I still believed she'd help me in a time of need so, with a deep breath, I asked her for help.

'I need to borrow some money,' I stuttered, with my head in my hands. 'I'm not coping.' I looked up to see her frowning at me.

'I can't lend you any money, Sam,' she replied bluntly, and my heart sank.

'I'm desperate.' My voice faltered and I willed myself not to cry, to pull it together, but Mum shook her head at me.

'I can't, Sam,' she said, and I nodded, defeated. There was no one else I could turn to but I couldn't bear the thought of having to meet up with older men again. I'll figure it out, I told myself. But I'm not going back down that road.

I moved to a new flat on London Street but that didn't solve my situation and things went from bad to worse. I felt humiliated as I was forced to steal food from shops. Whenever I was in the centre I'd see Amanda and we'd nod at each other as we passed by.

'Hi Sammy,' Amanda said to me one day.

'Alright,' I replied, not wanting to engage in a conversation with her.

'How's it going?' she asked and I shrugged.

'Same old,' I answered, averting her gaze. *Why would she care how I am?*

'If you ever need any work,' she offered, as she started to walk away, 'you know where to go.' I nodded.

'Laters,' I called out from over my shoulder. I went on with my day, trying to brush off her comment. Two or three parties would solve my problem, I thought, before shaking my head. But it's not worth it.

Over the next few days my gas and electric were switched off because I couldn't afford the bills. I was sitting in my front room one evening, mulling over what to do, when my phone rang in the kitchen. I ran over, picked it up, and instantly felt a lump in my throat. I would recognise that number anywhere. I clicked the answer button.

'Hey, Sammy!' Amanda chimed, as though we were still best friends. 'How are you?'

'Alright,' I replied blankly. I knew she couldn't possibly be ringing to see how I was. 'What's up?'

'Well . . .' She paused and I could tell she was after something. 'I've just moved to Birmingham, did you know that?'

'No, I didn't,' I admitted bluntly. I didn't know much about Amanda anymore.

'Yeah, well, fancy coming?'

'To Birmingham?'

'Yeah!' she exclaimed. 'I've got a job for you.'

'Ah.' I paused. I was desperate for any source of cash but I didn't want to venture round to grimy houses with her again. 'I don't know . . .' I wavered.

'But listen,' she jumped in. 'It's five hundred quid plus a shopping spree.' My jaw nearly hit the floor.

'Five hundred for one night?' I asked, unable to believe what I was hearing.

'Yeah, one night,' she clarified. 'Fancy it?' Suddenly my excitement faded. I battled with myself. I'd be mad to go along with it. I looked around my dark kitchen. I had no gas or electric, no food in the fridge – which was just as well because the fridge didn't even work.

'I don't know,' I replied. I felt trapped. I desperately wanted to turn my back on that way of life but I didn't know how else I could get money.

'Where are you living now?' she quizzed, and I gave her my address. 'There's a big Tesco near you, isn't there?'

'Yeah, there is.'

'Good, I thought so. I can get someone to come pick you up in the Tesco car park tomorrow night.' No, I thought to myself. I can't go through with it. I had promised myself I wouldn't do this again but it felt like I'd been left with no choice.

'Maybe,' I eventually replied, and I heard Amanda sigh.

'Right, well let me know,' she said, before hanging up.

I crumpled down onto the floor, nervously biting my lip. What else am I going to do? I despaired. I can't get a job, I can't rely on my family. The only person I had was Amanda. Through the past three years of knowing her, Amanda had made herself my entire world. She manipulated it so that I always leant on her and went to her when I needed something. No matter what the problem was, she always knew someone who could sort it out. If I don't go I'll either freeze or starve to death, I thought, too embarrassed to admit to Blaine how dire my situation was. With nowhere else to turn, I had no choice but to agree to Amanda's trip. I took out my phone and typed her a message: *I'll see you tomorrow.*

# 11.

# BIRMINGHAM

**M**aybe I should cancel Amanda's plans. I'd agreed to go just moments before and already I was having doubts. *I need the money but what if something terrible happens to me?* My stomach was twisting with painful anxiety and I winced. I had promised myself that I wouldn't do anything like this again, but looking around at my empty flat I knew I had no choice but to go through with it. I had been backed into a corner. The place was freezing and, as I sat alone shivering on the sofa, I decided I needed to text my youth worker. At least someone will know where I am, I told myself. Just in case.

I wrote: *I'm going away to Birmingham for a few days. If you don't hear from me, ring the police.* No sooner had I pressed send than I had an incoming call.

'What on earth is going on?' my youth worker asked. As

soon as she started speaking I panicked, unsure of what I should tell her.

'Nothing,' I lied, cringing as my voice squeaked. 'I'm just going to Birmingham.' *I can't tell her the truth.*

'But why are you going all the way to Birmingham?' she persisted. 'Your text has really concerned me, Samantha.'

'Just to chill,' I replied, racking my brains to try and come up with a plausible excuse. 'Because my friend's going,' I added.

'What's your friend's name?' she continued, and I knew by the tone of her voice that she didn't believe me. Suddenly I was stumped. I could hardly give her Amanda's name after I'd already reported her.

'Um, I don't remember,' I blurted out, losing control of my fabricated story. 'I have to go.' Before she could respond, I hung up the phone and, embarrassed, I threw it to the other side of the sofa. I couldn't bear to read her inevitable follow-up text. All I needed was for someone to know where I was going, I reassured myself. That's all that matters.

Satisfied that people would be looking for me if something went wrong, I went to sleep but, the next day, the knots in my stomach only tightened. Reluctantly I prepared to leave. Amanda had set it up so that when I reached the Tesco near my flat that evening, a black BMW would be waiting for me in the car park. As I headed out of the door, I picked up a knife from the kitchen and tucked it into my pocket. *So I can protect myself,* I thought and, with that, I left.

Just as she had planned, a black BMW was in the car

park. As I approached the car I noticed two Asian men sat in the front seats watching me. Be brave, I told myself, and walked up to them. When I got closer they both looked me up and down before one rolled down a window.

'Did Amanda send you?' I asked, leaning over the window as I spoke. 'I'm Sam.'

The driver glanced over at the other man before turning back. He nodded at me. 'Get in,' he said, gesturing towards the back seat. The men looked like they were in their mid-twenties and both of them had strong Brummie accents. I stepped into the back of the car, sliding into the middle seat. *Just so I can keep an eye on where we're going.* The ride was fairly quiet, with the two men making the odd comment to one another.

We had been driving on the motorway for over an hour when I realised I had no idea where we were. The road was dark, and the further we travelled in silence the more my heart raced. It's fine, I thought. I tried to calm myself down, holding on tight to the handle of the knife stashed in my pocket when, all of a sudden, we started to pull up onto the hard shoulder. I should have known this would happen, I panicked, convinced the men were going to attack me. Afterwards they'll ditch me on the side of the road, leaving me here to rot.

I listened anxiously while the pair of them whispered to one another but I couldn't make out what either of them was saying. The driver got out of the car and wandered off onto the grass to have a pee. The other guy then also left the car and, seizing my opportunity, I jumped into the driver's seat. It was pitch black, not that I knew how to drive anyway, and as soon as I was in the front, one of the men spotted me. He started yelling at me to get out.

'What's up?' he shouted, as he came running over.

'I know what you're going to do to me,' I shouted back. 'I'm not going to let it happen.'

'What are you on about?' The guy reached over and grabbed me by the shoulders.

'You're going to leave me here,' I told him.

'No I'm not,' he argued, as he wrestled to get me out of the driver's seat. 'Get out,' he ordered, his tone getting more aggressive. Grabbing my arms, he dragged me into the back seat. Petrified, I reached for my knife, my hand shaking as I held it out towards him.

'I'm not scared to stab you,' I tried to threaten, but my voice wavered. 'I will stab you.' I attempted to climb back into the front seat and, seething, the man grabbed me again, shoving me harder into the back. The other man joined him in the car and the pair of them stared at me spread across the seats. Hearing the child lock click into place, I let the knife go limp in my hand.

'I'm sorry,' I said pathetically, realising it was a fight I couldn't win. 'I'm scared,' I admitted. Without a word, the men turned back around and started the engine. We pulled back out onto the motorway.

'We're delivering you to Amanda,' the driver informed me after a few minutes of silence. 'Whether you like it or not.'

'Right,' I muttered, wishing I had never agreed to this.

'There's a guy there who wants to pay you five hundred pounds,' he added, and suddenly my ears pricked up.

'What?' I asked. 'One guy?' I couldn't believe it. For that kind of money I had assumed it would have been three or four men who wanted me to go to the party, not just one. *Maybe this won't be so bad. It might actually be easy.*

I figured with just one man I might even be allowed to leave after a couple of hours. I was so desperate for the money that I dismissed the nagging feeling I had that the offer seemed too good to be true. The men didn't respond to me and, after that, the car fell silent. Still on edge, I looked out for each road sign we passed, not relaxing until we reached Birmingham. We eventually pulled up in another car park.

One of the men opened the back door and they both led me into the Co-op, picking up beers for the party. The next time we stopped was when we reached a residential area. The car crawled around the neighbourhood for what felt like an eternity before we finally pulled up outside a house. I stepped out of the car, lingering behind the two men while they knocked on the door. Amanda answered, beaming at me as she let us into the house. She must be drunk, I noted, watching her sway from one side to the other. She knows I'm only here for the money.

Once inside, I couldn't believe how big the house was. I marvelled at the space, following Amanda into the massive living room. The front room held two sofas with a large fish tank standing in the corner. On the coffee table there lay a stash of booze and drugs. I noticed another girl sitting on a couch and I immediately recognised her from a care home we'd shared. I had been moved around so much over the years that it was hard to tell exactly which home it was, although neither of us let on that we knew each other.

'This is Stacey,' Amanda told me, and the pair of us nodded at one another. It seemed like Stacey was actively blanking me but I didn't care. My mind was focused on finding something to take so I didn't have to think about what was going to happen. I scanned the room, noticing there was only us three girls and the two men who had driven me there. I wonder who's paying me the £500, I thought, as I sat down on the floor beside Amanda.

In front of us was the coffee table where a hashish pipe stood beside a stash of cocaine and weed. Amanda began to draw out lines of the white powder but I didn't go near it. Instead I took some weed and sat cross-legged on the floor, rolling myself a joint. One of the men gave me a tour of the house before taking me back to the living room. He put on some reggae and, for a while, it was almost like a normal party. We all sat around laughing and joking with each other and I relaxed, to the extent that I even spent time using one of the men's laptops to log into Facebook.

When are they going to expect us to do stuff? I wondered, but no sooner had the thought crossed my mind than another man appeared at the door. He was also Asian but he looked older than the other two guys. He was fat and had uneven stubble on his face. He looks gross, I thought to myself. I saw Amanda glance from him to me and I knew this was the man I would have to have sex with. I picked up a bottle of vodka from the table and took a large swig. *I don't want to do this.*

'Are you coming, then?' the man said from the doorway, looking straight at me. I slowly rose from my spot and followed him into the bedroom. The room was bright and, as I looked around, I realised it must have been Stacey's actual bedroom. Her make-up lay across the dresser and girly pictures hung on the wall. There was a bed in the centre of the room and I noticed a single mattress on the floor. I started to make a beeline for the bed.

'Use the mattress,' I heard Stacey order. I spun around to find her at the doorway.

'Right,' I replied, letting her walk past me to sit herself down on the bed. 'Okay then.' My heart sank. This is the last time I do this, I promised myself. I can't go through this again. I looked at the mattress as I lowered myself onto it. It was blue with white stitching and surprisingly clean, thankfully. I lay still, watching the man as he lay down beside me. I knew what was coming next. Right, I told myself. You need to get this over with. I just wanted to get paid and get as far away from Amanda as possible so, reluctantly, I unbuttoned his trousers.

Stacey turned the light off and I was grateful she had; the last thing I wanted to see was this guy's ugly face. As he raped me, I stared blankly at the ceiling. I didn't even know his name but I didn't care. I just wanted my £500 so I could go home. He was vile, crushing me with his weight. I noticed there was a large marking that ran diagonally across his back. It was almost like he had been hit with a belt at some point and it had scarred. I let myself focus on wondering how he'd got the scar rather than what was happening.

I couldn't understand why he was offering me so much money. It was nothing out of the ordinary for Amanda's parties and I was rarely given more than £50. I could hear Stacey having sex on the bed with someone else. Is she one of Amanda's girls too? I wondered. The man was rough with me and I winced as the ordeal seemed to last forever. When it was finally over he rolled off me and got up, leaving the bedroom without a word. I didn't move. Instead, I held my breath, willing myself to disappear. What the fuck, I thought. Why can't I escape this?

Eventually I wandered back into the living room. The man I'd just slept with was nowhere to be seen but I was shocked to find Amanda in the front room having sex with two men. Her over-the-top moans made me want to laugh and, not knowing where else to go, I sat down to roll myself another joint and wait for her to be finished.

'Mucky bum,' I quipped when she finally looked at me, but she ignored me, pushing past to snort a line of coke on the table. The men she had been with left the room and, once she'd used up the last of the cocaine, she stood up.

'I'm going for a shower,' she announced, before heading

to the bathroom. I gave her a small nod, picking up the unfinished bottle of vodka. *The night will go quicker if I'm drunk.* I was alone in the living room for no longer than five minutes when the older man I had been with re-emerged. He sat down beside me on the sofa, touching my thigh creepily. I grimaced. I knew all too well what he expected of me. I lay down on the sofa and closed my eyes. This time it was over quickly. Afterwards he stayed on top of me and I squirmed, trying to wriggle free. Hearing Amanda leave the bathroom, I took my chance to excuse myself.

'I'm going to have a shower now, if you don't mind,' I said. His weight on my chest made it hard for me to breathe.

'Yeah sure,' he replied, sitting up. 'You know where it is.'

I left him in the living room and made my way to the bathroom. Walking past the open bedroom door, I spotted Amanda lying down to sleep on the mattress I'd had sex on earlier. Gross. I left her to it, finding solace in the bathroom as I started to run the water. I had thought this night would have been easy but as soon as I stepped into the shower I began to cry. I was shocked that I was getting so upset, but once I'd started sobbing I couldn't stop. I scrubbed uncontrollably at my skin, unable to rid myself of the man's smell. My skin crawled, almost itchy, and I was repulsed by the thought of being touched.

My mind wandered to Blaine and how kind he had always been to me. Am I cheating on him? I wondered, horrified at the idea. We were on and off like always but this was the first time I'd had sex for money since meeting him. It's okay, I tried to convince myself. I'll use the money I get for tonight on food and bills and then whatever's left I can spend on visiting Blaine. But then I realised that Blaine might question where I'd got the money from and I started to feel sick. I let the water run for a while longer as I closed my eyes, pretending I was at home, but, eventually, I had to face reality.

I turned off the shower and then noticed the only towel in the room was lying crumpled on the floor. I gingerly picked it up. It was filthy and soaking wet. I'm not using that, I thought. It's disgusting. Instead I perched myself on the edge of the bath and lit a cigarette. I took a few drags, staring at the towel on the laminate floor, and zoned out, waiting until I had dried off. Then I got dressed and crept back into the living room. The man was already fast asleep on the sofa we'd had sex on. I sighed. I guess I'm not getting my money tonight then, I realised. I'll have to wait until the morning. I curled up on the other sofa and willed the night to end.

The next morning I was woken by the sun glaring through a crack in the curtains. I sat up, burying my head in my hands. Last night's drinking had taken full effect in the form of a hangover. I peered over at the couch next to mine and was suddenly wide awake. *Where's that man gone?* He had been there last night but now I was alone. I ran off in search of him around the house as the horror started to dawn on me. *All the men from last night are gone.* I peeked into the bedroom and could see Amanda and

Stacey asleep. I realised it was just the three of us left in the house. Don't panic, I told myself. Amanda will know what to do. Frantic, I waited impatiently in the living room for her to wake up.

'Where's my money?' I quizzed her, as soon she appeared. She pulled a face as if I'd asked her something nonsensical.

'What money?' Amanda retorted, reaching for a cigarette on the table before leaving the room. *Don't play games with me,* I wanted to scream, following her through to the kitchen.

'My five hundred pounds,' I reminded her. Amanda was silent as she lit her cig.

'You've already got it,' she replied. Amanda had stopped making eye contact with me.

'No I haven't,' I argued. 'Amanda, search me right now, I haven't got it.' I pulled at my empty pockets but she didn't bother to look. I could feel my eyes start to well up. *I need this money to appear now.*

'Well,' Amanda paused, as if mulling over her response, 'tough.'

'Tough?' I repeated in shock. 'How am I meant to get back to Sheffield?' Amanda shrugged and I was lost for words. But I was relying on that money, I despaired. This was all for nothing. I was furious and I wanted to hit her but, overwhelmed by my upset, instead I fled. I knew full well I would break down in tears if I stayed a second longer. I stormed down the street, not stopping until I was at the end of the road. I looked around, having no clue where I was. I didn't even know which direction I needed to walk in. *Where am I supposed to go?* Unable to hold it together any longer, I threw myself down in the middle of the pavement and burst into tears. *This is rock bottom.* Not knowing what else to do, I took out my phone and rang my youth worker.

'My friend's ditched me,' I told her, trying to keep my voice steady. I couldn't bring myself to tell her the full story. 'I'm a bit stuck.'

'Samantha, you've gone there voluntarily,' my care worker sighed. 'I can't pick you up.' I hung up, defeated. Deep down I knew that if I'd told her the real reason why I was there, she would have come to get me, but I couldn't do it. I looked up and down the unfamiliar street and dialled the only number I could think to call: 999.

'I came to Birmingham with a friend and now they've left me in the lurch,' I wailed. I couldn't believe it had come to this. 'I'm sixteen and I'm a care leaver.' I think they must have taken pity on me because they sent a police car to pick me up.

'Are you alright?' one of the officers asked, as I got into the car.

'Yeah,' I lied, sitting myself down. 'I'm just lost.' They drove me to a nearby police station where they interviewed me. I refused to back down on my made-up story, explaining over and over again how my friend had left me on my own, and so, after an hour, they took me to the closest train station. At first, the staff at the station didn't want to let me on the train for free, and it took convincing from the police for them to finally give me a travel card. I boarded the train back to Sheffield, tears streaming down my face. What in the world am I going to do now? I thought, watching trees whizz past the window.

Back in the city, I made my way down my street and the high-rise block of flats loomed over me. Once home, I couldn't believe how cold it had become. I breathed into my hands to warm them as I sat down on the sofa. I still didn't have any gas or electric and I had no idea how I was going to get the money together to reconnect it. I felt my phone buzz and, looking at the screen, I saw I had a number of missed calls from Amanda. Seething, I threw my phone across the room, letting it smash against a wall.

That night cemented to me that Amanda was not my friend. I didn't want to hang out with her anymore and I had no interest in being cool. I hated her. I borrowed money from a neighbour to pay my bills but that only landed me in more debt. Unable to find another way to make money, I used more trips to houses to pay it off. I was addicted to the lifestyle Amanda had groomed me to endure – the free drugs and booze was not only a perk of the parties but it was how I coped. I despised the life I was leading but it was a downward spiral that I couldn't control. I was trapped.

# 12.

# AMANDA'S PREGNANT

I didn't see Amanda for a few weeks after the Birmingham incident, not that it bothered me; I was glad of the break. I didn't want to spend time with her anymore. By now, I didn't need Amanda to send me off to the parties. I knew full well which houses I could find work in. Selling my body for sex made me feel ill, and every night I'd crawl back into bed and wish I could be anybody else but me. But the promise of drugs and alcohol was too great to resist and I relied on them more and more.

The next time I saw Amanda was by chance. I was out in the city centre shopping for food when, as I walked down the street, I realised I was heading straight for her. She was standing talking to someone I didn't recognise, hands stuffed into her body warmer with her classic oversized hoops dangling from her ears. As I got closer she clocked me and immediately turned her back. I shrugged it off. I don't want to speak to her anyway, I thought, intending to storm past without a second look. But as I approached I caught a glance of her figure from the side. *Blimey*, I marvelled to myself. Amanda had always been stick thin and I couldn't help but notice her stomach protruding from her jacket. *She's really put on weight.* I shook my head as I marched past, leaving her behind, but, that night, I went home and couldn't shake her from my thoughts. How on earth has she got so big? I asked myself, almost laughing at the idea of Amanda gaining weight. She was so self-obsessed that it felt like karma, but something about it just didn't add up. I sat down in my tiny living room, trying to forget about her, when suddenly it clicked – *Amanda's pregnant!*

I couldn't believe it but suddenly it all made sense. *That's why she ignored me, she's embarrassed.* I smirked. Amanda had long since lost my sympathy but I couldn't wait to see her to find out the details. I kept an eye out for her whenever I was in the city centre and, a few days later, I spotted her loitering outside Savers. There was no mistaking the obvious bump under her shirt as I made a beeline for her, not giving her the chance to run off.

'Pregnant, are we?' I asked, my voice higher than intended. I had tried to restrain the smug feeling I had but I couldn't hide it. She looked blankly at me, as if in shock, before responding.

'Um...' she hesitated, before looking down at her stomach. 'Yeah, I am.'

'Alright then,' I replied. Amanda didn't have a maternal bone in her body and she was the last person I ever expected to have a baby. 'Who's the father?'

'I don't know,' she admitted. After all the lies she had told over the years, I wasn't sure whether to believe her or not, but she was adamant. At first I was almost glad she was pregnant, as though it could act as some form of justice for what she had done, but then the reality washed over me and I felt a lump form in my throat. Eventually there was going to be an innocent baby in the mix and it would have only Amanda to take care of it. Does this baby really deserve a mother like her? I asked myself, horrified.

'Do you know what you're having?' I quizzed, after a few seconds of silence.

'A boy,' she answered. Poor baby, I thought. I knew she could never be a proper mother to him.

'Right,' I concluded, not knowing what else to say. 'Well, good luck then.' I left her there and headed towards the nearby tram stop. This baby is her problem, not mine, I tried to tell myself, as I walked away, but I couldn't ignore the growing feeling of guilt I had. The baby hadn't asked to be born. I battled internally. I knew all too well what it was like growing up with an uncaring mum. As I made my way down the road, I passed a B&M and felt compelled to go in. I stared at the different Babygros hanging up in the aisle. I'll just pick up a few things, I decided. They're for the baby, not her.

The next day I spotted Amanda at the markets. She was

surrounded as usual by a group of men, and as I approached I noticed she had a can of cider in one hand and a cigarette in the other. I felt my cheeks flush with anger but I didn't say anything, instead focusing on the baby clothes I was carrying.

'Here you go.' I presented them to her and watched as her face lit up. 'Just to get you started.'

'Cheers, pal.' She beamed, resting the cig in her mouth to take them. She lifted up the Babygro to get a better look. 'They're great.'

She stuffed the clothes into her bag before turning back to her hangers-on. I gave her a nod and, with that, I left. I've done my bit now, I told myself. It's not my baby. After everything she had put me through I wanted to see her struggle but I still had a niggling feeling that I should help her. If Amanda wasn't pregnant I would have happily never spoken to her again but I felt sorry for the child, knowing he was going to have her as a mum. I couldn't sit back and do nothing. I felt like I had a duty of care to the child.

Taking an interest in her pregnancy, I started chatting to her whenever we saw each other in the city centre, although it wasn't long before she started hinting for help.

'Social services have been breathing down my neck,' she complained one afternoon. 'You know, there's such a lot of stuff they want me to get for the kid.'

'Oh, really?' I asked, concerned about her baby. 'What have they said?'

'Well, a social worker told me that I'm not going to be able to keep the baby if I don't have a cot,' she continued, looking down at her bump before staring back at me. 'There's so much I need to get but I just don't have the money.'

I could see past her false worry, knowing full well that underneath all of the complaints she was really just asking me to get the things for her. Even so, I couldn't help but buy into the guilt trips. How is she so unprepared? I wondered, as she reeled off the list of items she needed. Amanda was short on a pram, a Moses basket, clothes – and she expected me to get them for her.

'I'll see what I can pick up,' I offered, and at first she was happy with that. Whenever I was at the shops I made sure to get something for her but I couldn't afford the bigger items she was looking for. Deep down, I wanted to take the baby off her and raise him myself. I thought I'd be a far better mum than Amanda could ever be. I couldn't bear the thought of her dragging up a child. She was still drinking and smoking, after all – she didn't deserve this baby. Although she never told me, I suspected she was still prostituting while she was pregnant and the thought of it made me want to be sick. I don't want that for the baby, I thought, and I started to give her some of my benefit money in the hopes that she'd stop.

'This isn't going to do,' she moaned one day, looking through the toys and blankets I'd bought for her. 'Social services won't care about this.' We were sat down on a bench in the Peace Gardens and Amanda's bump was looking bigger than ever. Instead of being excited about her baby, she only ever talked about the things she needed to buy. She never seemed to have any real emotion.

'I can't buy you the other stuff,' I reminded her. *How does she expect me to pay for her Moses basket and pram?*

'Maybe I should start shoplifting them,' she said slowly, looking at me. It was as if she wanted me to tell her not to.

'Go on, then,' I replied nonchalantly. I had given up trying to help her. Whatever I did wasn't good enough but I knew I couldn't stop Amanda from shoplifting.

'I'm pregnant though, Sammy,' she replied, giving me a pathetic look. 'If I go to prison I'm going to lose my kid.'

'Right,' I answered, not wanting to make eye contact with her. I had a sinking feeling in the pit of my stomach and I guessed where she was going with this.

'So, can you?' She raised her eyebrows expectantly. 'Just this one time.'

'I can't go back inside,' I blurted out, remembering the weeks spent in New Hall. I was in no hurry to return.

'But if I do it and get caught,' she paused, waiting for me to look her in the eye, 'the kid will be taken by social services.' She knew how to tug on my heartstrings. I can't let this kid go into care, I argued with myself. I've been there, and I wouldn't wish that on him. I saw Amanda's baby as a fresh start for her, even a chance to wipe the slate clean. I knew what it was like to grow up in care and I didn't want this baby to suffer the same fate.

'Fine,' I agreed. As an unofficial auntie to this little boy, I knew what I had to do. I had made it my mission to make sure he had everything he could ever want before he was even born. It's not the baby's fault, I thought. If his mum won't look out for him, then I will.

Reluctantly I started to shoplift for Amanda, and at first I thought I was just doing it as a favour, but the reality was I was still trapped by her. Am I ever going to get Amanda out of my life? I wondered. It seemed that no matter what she did to me there was always something that drew me back in. I missed the times when I thought she was my best friend, and even though they were false I deeply missed the sense of belonging I used to have with her. Maybe this baby can change her, I hoped. It might make her want to be a better person.

After a few months of stealing for her, I headed into town one day with more goods for her but she was nowhere to be found. After searching for an hour, I spotted a familiar face sat down by the markets.

'Hey, Olivia,' I called out, waving, and she looked up at me. 'Have you seen Amanda anywhere?'

'Ah, she's in hospital,' Olivia confirmed, rolling up a fag on the floor. 'She's had the baby.'

'Wow,' I replied. 'That's great.' I hesitated before adding, 'Did she get to keep him?'

Olivia laughed, shaking her head. 'Of course she couldn't keep it,' she answered, fishing a lighter out of her pocket. 'There was never any doubt about that.'

She lit her cigarette and took a drag. I was stunned. Olivia had to be right. If the day Amanda gave birth was the same day her little boy was taken into care, then she'd never had any chance of keeping him, I thought bitterly. The only consolation I had was that this baby had at least been given a chance of a normal life away from Amanda. Hopefully, wherever he is, he's loved and appreciated. That was something Amanda would never have done for him. I felt stupid for falling for her lies once again. All I wanted was to move on with my life and not have anything to do with her, but that seemed impossible. Oh well, I sighed. I just needed to forget about her.

Pushing Amanda to the back of my mind, I continued to attend parties on my own, often getting so drunk that I woke up having no idea where I was. Sometimes I'd wake up and realise I wasn't even at a house anymore; I'd be in the public toilets of a park or lying face down in a bush. I would stumble home, my crotch stinging, and I would have no idea what had happened to me.

One night, as a man raped me on a bare bedroom floor, I started to fade in and out of consciousness. It was like a movie, flicking between the man and total darkness. Paralysed on the ground, I couldn't move my head and I started to panic. A sick smile spread across the man's face as he writhed on top of me. I squirmed, struggling to breathe under his weight. My head pounded with what felt like the worst headache in the world. I realised I needed water, and looked over at a bottle that was just out of reach. When will this end? I wanted to cry, but then everything faded to black.

# AMANDA'S PREGNANT

When I awoke it was daylight and I was alone. What even happened last night? I wondered, clutching my forehead. In a daze, I crept past the empty booze bottles and fled from the house. On the sobering walk home I vowed to escape the lifestyle I was leading. If I don't stop now, I'll die, I told myself.

A few days later I had to attend a meeting with a social worker to discuss my housing. This was a regular occurrence if I needed to be moved or if my benefits were changing. I usually brought Mum along to fight my case with them, and today was no exception.

'Sam needs her care leavers' grant,' Mum informed the social worker, as I sat silently beside her. My mum had always been better with the legal jargon than me, but we hadn't even been there five minutes when there was a knock at the door.

'Come in,' my social worker said, waving some people through to the office. My jaw dropped when I saw it was two police officers.

'What have you done now, Sam?' Mum accused me, but I shook my head.

'Nothing,' I protested. My mind raced back to the shoplifting I'd done for Amanda's baby.

'It's nothing to worry about,' one of the officers reassured us. 'We're here about an allegation you've made.'

'What allegation—' Mum started to ask, before I interrupted.

'Mum, you need to go now,' I pleaded. I knew how nosy

she was and I desperately didn't want her listening in, but she wouldn't move from her spot. The officer ignored her and turned back to face me.

'We want to talk to you about an allegation you made against Amanda Spencer.'

# 13.

# SEEKING JUSTICE

Sitting in my social worker's office I couldn't believe what I was hearing. When I'd left prison after reporting Amanda to my counsellor, I had assumed nothing would be done about my allegations. By now I was used to people letting me down, but here I was, sat before two police officers who wanted to listen to what I had to say.

'My name is Paul Badger,' one of them said, reaching out to shake my hand. He was middle-aged, and the first thing I noticed was how tall he was. Paul Badger towered over me as I sat, arms crossed, in the office chair.

'Can you tell us a bit about your friendship with Amanda?' he asked, giving me a reassuring smile. Thinking back to the times I'd spent with her, I felt too embarrassed to talk to him directly about it. The female officer at his side seemed less intimidating so, ignoring Paul, I focused on speaking to her.

'She used to get me to go to parties,' I muttered, ashamed to acknowledge what we'd done together.

'What kind of parties did Amanda take you to?' Paul went on. He was like a giant stood next to me but his calm voice was helping me feel at ease.

'Sex parties,' I admitted, my cheeks burning with embarrassment. The officers wanted to know more but I didn't want to go into detail, especially with Mum there. What will they think of me if I tell them? I worried. I tried to stutter out a sentence but, every time I went to speak, I felt my mum's eyes watching me and I clammed up.

'Was it rape?' Paul finally asked over the silence. 'Or was it consensual?'

'Um…' I paused, not knowing what to say. Deep down I knew what had happened with the older men wasn't consensual, but a small part of me felt guilty for admitting it. I had been conditioned to believe I deserved the abuse I'd received, but now was my chance to right those wrongs.

'Rape,' I eventually whispered, and immediately felt a rush of relief. It was like I had voiced a secret I'd been holding in forever, but it didn't stop Paul's questions. He wanted to know how old I was at the time and who had been behind the parties.

'Who handed you the money afterwards?' he continued to quiz.

'Amanda,' I told him, but the more I divulged, the more I started to panic. Amanda is going to kill me if she finds out, I thought. I can't afford to be revealing so much information.

'Look,' I blurted out amongst the questions. 'I don't want to be involved.'

'But we could really use your help with this–' Paul started to say before I interrupted.

'I'll tell you this stuff now but if it goes to trial then I'm not giving evidence,' I warned. 'If my name gets mentioned, I'll deny everything.' I was too scared of what the consequences could be if I fought Amanda on this. I knew by now that Amanda herself was too cowardly to confront me, but I had no idea how the men from the houses would react if I started to make allegations against them. Unable to persuade me otherwise, Paul agreed that I wouldn't have to testify against her and, after that, I spoke to him for about half an hour. I gave the officers minimal detail on what Amanda and I had got up to, vividly aware of my mum listening to every word I was saying.

'Thanks, Samantha.' Paul Badger shook my hand before giving me a piece of paper. 'If you change your mind about speaking out, this is my number.' He smiled briefly as the pair of them headed out. I tucked the paper into my pocket. That's never going to happen, I thought. People like me don't get justice.

I tried to brush off the conversation I'd just had, ignoring my mum's incessant questioning. Deep down I wished I could have been brave enough to tell the police everything, but I couldn't bring myself to do it and there was no point in dwelling on something I couldn't change. I pushed it to the back of my mind and, a few days later, I made my way to the markets to pick up some baccy. With my head down, focusing on the feet in front of me, I tried to go unnoticed.

'Hi, Sammy,' a voice called out and I froze. Please don't let that be Amanda, I thought to myself, and was relieved when I turned around to find another girl standing in front of me. I vaguely recognised her as someone who hung around Amanda from time to time, but the pair of us had barely spoken until today.

'Hey,' I answered, giving her a quick smile. I was reluctant to stop and chat, not wanting to bump into anyone else.

'Have you seen Amanda?' she asked me, and I groaned.

'No,' I replied, rolling my eyes. I hated that people still associated me with her. It felt like no matter what I did I couldn't shake her off. Are we always going to be Samanda? I thought, cringing at the term.

'Oh,' the girl continued. 'So have you heard about Bunny?' Immediately my ears pricked up at the sound of a familiar name.

'No,' I replied, remembering the blonde girl I'd met in prison who had opened my eyes to what Amanda was really like. 'What's happened to Bunny?'

'I don't know if it's true,' she paused, lowering her voice, 'but there's a rumour going round that she killed herself.' My jaw dropped open. I'd only known Bunny for a short time but I knew all too well the abuse Amanda had let her suffer. My mind raced back to the things Bunny had told me when we were in the young offenders unit together. Had this happened because of what she'd been through?

'How do you know?' I stuttered, almost at a loss for words. The girl shrugged.

'I'm not entirely sure how true it is, but that's what everyone's saying.' In shock, I didn't respond. Instead I nodded, glancing over to the baccy man perched on a nearby stall.

'I've got to go,' I excused myself. There was no way of knowing if the rumours about Bunny were true, but the idea haunted me. *If Bunny is dead then it's Amanda's fault – she's to blame.* I realised I couldn't hide from what Amanda had done any longer. What had happened to me was in the past, but Amanda's actions were still hurting people. It's time to grow up, I told myself. I need to be mature about this. I didn't want any part in Amanda's world anymore. I needed to shake her off for good this time.

Over the next few days I mulled over what to do. Revisiting the piece of paper the police officer had given to me, I took a deep breath. Can I really go through with testifying against Amanda? I wondered, putting the paper back down on the kitchen counter. Probably not, I concluded. But it wasn't long before my phone rang.

'Hi Samantha, it's Paul Badger here.'

'Oh,' I answered, surprised he was ringing me. 'Hi.' *Was this a sign?*

'Listen,' Paul started, quickly cutting to the chase. 'If we are to have any hope of convicting Amanda, we really need you to give evidence. I know you're worried about it all but we need your help and we'll be by your side the entire time.'

I smiled. Paul's plea was exactly what I'd wanted to hear. The shocking news about Bunny was the kick I had needed to finally do something about Amanda and, for the first time, I felt ready to get justice.

'Okay,' I agreed. 'I'll do it.' I told Paul I would meet him at the police station but I was a bag of nerves as I made my way down there to give my statement. I hope I'm doing the right thing, I worried, as my stomach twisted into knots.

Paul greeted me at the reception before showing me to an interview room. It was plain, with just a table and two chairs occupying the space. Next to one chair stood a camera and that's where Paul positioned himself, focusing the camera onto me. I nervously sat myself down.

'Are you ready?' he asked, and I nodded, watching as he hit 'record'. 'How did you first meet Amanda Spencer?'

'In town one day,' I replied, shifting in my seat. 'She took us shoplifting.'

'Who were you with that day?' he asked, holding a stack of notes in front of him.

'My brother,' I answered. I told Paul about the things we shoplifted and about the times Amanda and I would sit and laugh at the city centre markets.

'How old were you when she introduced you to the parties?' he quizzed me. This was the part I had been dreading.

'Thirteen years old,' I told him bluntly.

'And was it always Amanda who took you to them?' Paul continued, and I nodded. 'So, what would happen at the parties?'

I shrugged. 'Just sex,' I remarked, trying to seem nonchalant. I struggled to admit how I really felt about the ordeal.

'And you were thirteen when you had sex at the parties?' he clarified, and again I nodded. I was starting to get impatient with his repetitive questions. 'How old were the men?'

'All ages,' I answered, shifting restlessly in the chair. My voice was monotone. 'Twenties, thirties, forties . . . maybe older.' Paul sat dead still, looking at me. 'Amanda took me all the time; she liked that she could get me to do stuff.'

It was the first time I'd ever said any of these things out loud and, at first, the interview felt like the toughest thing I'd ever done, but once I started opening up I couldn't stop. I rambled through the various incidents, the abuse I had endured and the house in Birmingham. Every now and then Paul would have to tell me to slow down or repeat something I'd stumbled over.

'What about the men at those houses,' Paul started to ask me. 'Do you remember what they looked like?' I didn't have much information on them, and the little I did have I didn't want to share.

'Does it matter?' I retorted, my cheeks flushed. 'They were just faceless men.' I wanted justice for what had happened to the other girls, especially Bunny, but to do that I figured I had to focus on Amanda. Anyone else I talk about is just a distraction from the real criminal, I told myself. While before I had been scared of her, I now knew that Amanda couldn't hurt me anymore. I was stronger than her and I was going to take her down.

After my interview I returned to the city centre to find that rumours about Amanda were flying everywhere. Everyone I usually spoke to in town was talking about the abuse allegations.

'I've heard of other girls being abused because of her,' someone mentioned to me at the markets. 'There's plenty of girls out there who haven't come forward.'

'Likely is,' I agreed, and the comment struck a chord with me. That's probably truer than anybody even realises, I thought, knowing I had an opportunity to do something. Determined to get justice, I took the picture I had of Amanda from my purse and brought it with me the next time I was heading into the centre. I knew there had to be other girls around Sheffield who she had abused and I was going to make it my mission to find them. I wandered through the markets, the Peace Gardens and to the groups of teenagers standing outside the bookies. I stopped by a group of young girls.

'Do you know Amanda Spencer?' I asked, showing them the passport-sized picture of her.

'I've seen her before,' one of them admitted, glancing at the picture.

'Have you heard the rumours, then?' I continued, passing the photo amongst them. 'Do you know what she's done?'

'Yeah, we've heard the rumours,' the girl replied, handing the picture back to me. 'But we don't know if it's true.'

'Come on,' I protested. 'You know what she's done.' But the girl shook her head. Defeated, I moved on. The next three days were spent wandering around the city centre clutching Amanda's picture. I was convinced there had to be some girls out there who had been affected by what she had done, but by the time I spoke to a group of girls near the markets, I had all but given up hope.

'No, sorry,' one of them said, as she handed me back my photo. 'I don't know anything.' As I turned to leave, I couldn't help but notice how one of the other girls hung behind the rest, not wanting to acknowledge what I was asking. I vaguely recognised her as a young girl named Poppy. She was tall and slim with dark blonde hair and I had previously seen her speaking to Amanda. I let the girls leave without a word, but the next time I spotted Poppy she was on her own outside Wilko.

'Do you fancy a chat?' I asked, walking up to her. She looked shocked but agreed to walk with me to the Peace Gardens. 'I know what you've been doing for Amanda,' I added, lowering my voice.

'I haven't done anything,' Poppy insisted, as we made our way to the gardens.

'I know you have,' I repeated, giving her a light pat on the back. We plonked ourselves down on the damp grass and I watched as she absentmindedly picked at the weeds by our feet. I could tell by the way she fidgeted uncomfortably that she had something to tell me and, eventually, Poppy looked up.

'It happened to me,' she said quietly, 'with Amanda.' I nodded understandingly and, for a while, neither of us said anything.

'It's going to be okay,' I whispered finally. 'It's not your fault.' When Poppy didn't respond, I hesitated before adding, 'You have to come forward.'

'I can't,' she snapped back, shaking her head. The helpless look in her eye felt all too familiar.

'But you're not on your own,' I tried to reassure her. 'There's other girls just like you speaking out.' I was desperate for more girls to band together against Amanda. I wanted her to know that I would be there to help her but I knew I couldn't make her come forward. She had to be ready herself – I couldn't be ready for her.

'I'll think about it,' Poppy concluded, ending our conversation. I left her that afternoon wondering if all my efforts had been for nothing. Were they all too frightened of Amanda to speak out? A few days later, I had a call from Paul Badger.

Paul had been working round the clock on the case to bring Amanda to justice and, when I answered, he was in high spirits.

'I've got some good news,' he announced.

'What is it?' I asked, excited to finally hear something positive.

'More girls have come forward against Amanda,' he told me, and I beamed.

'That's great,' I exclaimed, listening to how there were now at least seven new victim statements.

'This is really going to help our case,' Paul chirped. After I hung up the phone, I couldn't stop smiling. I felt happy to know that those girls deciding to speak out could have possibly been down to me and it gave me a new sense of purpose. I knew I couldn't change the past. I couldn't save those girls from abuse they had already suffered at the hands of Amanda – but I could change our future, and I was going to make sure Amanda didn't take advantage of another vulnerable girl ever again.

## 14.

# JORDAN

Alongside the case that was building against Amanda, I was still on and off with Blaine, seeing him from time to time if he visited Sheffield. I made the decision to keep most of the police investigation away from him, wanting to treat the time we spent together as an escape. Every now and then, if I could scrape the money together, I would go down to Chesterfield for the week to see him. But it wasn't until the springtime of 2012 that something potentially life-changing dawned on me: it had easily been two months since my last period. I was nineteen years old and petrified. In total denial, I didn't know where to turn. I can't tell Blaine unless I'm sure, I decided. With no one else to confide in, I swallowed my pride and went round to my mum's house.

'I'm late,' I winced, as I told her. We had been nattering

on her sofa while I procrastinated, having no idea how she would react, but Mum didn't bat an eyelid.

'I'll buy a test then,' she offered, getting up to leave and, the next thing I knew, I was sat alone in her bathroom waiting for the results. Perched on the lid of the toilet seat, I clutched the wand with both hands, my eyes squeezed shut. This can't be happening, I convinced myself – the test has to be negative. The idea that I could be expecting was almost ludicrous but when I opened my eyes I was met with two telltale pink lines – I was pregnant.

'Mum!' I shouted, running out into the hallway. 'Look.' I pushed the test towards her, and for a moment we both stood in silence.

'Well,' Mum said finally, handing the device back to me, 'I guess you're having a baby.'

I couldn't believe it and I didn't. For the first couple of months I was in complete and utter denial. But something that pains me more than anything else to admit was that I continued to get drunk and use drugs during my pregnancy. It was as if I had given up on life all together, like the pregnancy was a nightmare and alcohol made it disappear. I continued to attend parties, getting myself so intoxicated that I had no idea where I was. I thought I could drink my problems away but I was wrong. I hadn't received any counselling for my ordeal with Amanda and, unable to deal with my trauma, I had what social services described as a 'chaotic lifestyle'. Living in and out of homeless shelters and associating with drug dealers wasn't in any way a suitable environment to raise a child and, as soon as they discovered I was pregnant, my unborn baby was put on the at-risk register.

'I don't know what I'm doing,' I cried to my social worker. I couldn't imagine ever being stable enough to be a parent. Social services tried to help me but I felt myself slipping into a downward spiral. I knew if I told Blaine it would make the pregnancy real when all I wanted was for it to vanish. For a while I ignored my growing bump, drinking and partying as normal until, one day, everything changed.

I was lying on my sofa one evening, looking down in shock at how much my small bump had grown when, suddenly, I felt it – a tiny kick out of nowhere sparked goosebumps that ran along my arms.

'Oh my God,' I shouted audibly, clutching my stomach. 'I'm having a baby!' A baby that needs me. That was all it took, a nudge in the right direction from my own baby to push me back on track. *I can't carry on like this, I need to do something.* I sprang into action almost instantly, determined to be the mother any baby deserved.

I knew I had to do the right thing, and Blaine was still none the wiser so, reluctantly, I paid the necessary visit to Chesterfield to see him. I took a seat in his living room, my bump hidden under a jacket. Then I took a deep breath.

'Um,' I started to say, hesitating. 'There's something I have to tell you.' I paused, and Blaine looked at me, waiting. 'I'm pregnant,' I blurted out, louder than I'd intended.

'You liar,' Blaine barked back, laughing. He shook his head in amusement and started rolling himself a cigarette.

'I'm not,' I insisted. How could I convince him I was telling the truth? I had once before lied about being pregnant to stop Blaine from leaving me, so it was no wonder he didn't believe me now. It took a while to convince him, refusing to give in when he told me to stop lying. Once he finally realised I was telling the truth, he was lost for words.

'Oh, right,' he muttered, and I could tell he was in shock. 'Right, okay.'

'I just thought you should know,' I replied, not knowing what else to say.

'Yeah,' Blaine answered, looking down at his rolled cigarette. 'Thanks.' I wasn't sure if he still had doubts but I kept him at arm's length after that, only messaging him about the baby when I needed to. My only focus now was on making sure I found somewhere to live for my baby. I was set on doing things properly, agreeing to a meeting with social services. But sat in the stuffy office with my social worker was where I was delivered the bad news.

'After the birth, the baby will be placed in immediate foster care,' the social worker informed me. 'And after that the situation will be assessed and you will be given supervised visitation.' I was devastated.

'But what if I've got my act together by then?' I begged, not ready to give up. 'I'm trying to find somewhere nice to live.' I wanted to prove I could be responsible enough to take good care of my baby but the social worker just shook her head.

'I'm really sorry but it's too late at this point,' she confirmed, sifting through the paperwork on her desk. 'Right now your life is too chaotic to be suitable for a baby.' I didn't want to believe what I was hearing. I could be a good mum, I thought. They don't know how good I'd be with a baby.

Running out of options, I started to consider fleeing town. They can't put the baby into care if they can't find us, I told myself and, looking around my dingy flat, I realised there was nothing to keep me where I was. In a desperate attempt to stop social services from taking my baby away, I made the move away from Sheffield back to my childhood hometown of Grimsby. I hadn't been back to Grimsby in years, but my nan still lived in the area and I moved just around the corner from her, on Pasture Street. I thought that if I found somewhere nice to live, then by some miracle I'd be allowed to keep the baby, so I concentrated on preparing for the arrival.

All notion of Amanda and the case Paul Badger was working on went out of the window and I didn't care if I never heard Amanda's name again. Meanwhile, Nan and I bonded over the pregnancy. She took me out shopping to buy me baby clothes and I brought pictures from the scans round to the house to show her. We loved talking about the future, imagining what the baby would be like or grow up to become.

'I wonder if it's a girl or a boy,' I contemplated over a cup of tea one afternoon.

# PIMPED

'Me too,' my nana said, giving my swollen belly a rub. 'But either way, I can't wait to meet them.' I smiled. Having Nan back in my life provided a welcome sense of stability.

The housing association I was living with in Grimsby had appointed me a support worker, Joy, and she attended most of my baby scans for moral support.

'Are you ready?' she asked, as I answered the door to her.

'As I'll ever be,' I replied, giving her a grin. Today was the day of my gender scan and, as Joy drove us both to the nearby hospital, I sat in silence, giddy with excitement at the prospect.

'It'll definitely feel real after today,' Joy chirped from behind the wheel, and I smiled, nodding.

'I know,' I agreed, stroking my bump. 'I can't wait.' Once we got to the hospital I waited impatiently for my name to be called. What's taking them so long? I thought anxiously, but I finally found myself being led into a small room.

'Do you want to lie down?' a nurse asked, pointing towards the bed. With a mixture of nerves and excitement, I sat back and looked over at Joy. She gave me a thumbs up. The sonographer walked into the room and introduced herself.

'Let's find out what you're having,' she said, and I wriggled as she applied the cold gel to my belly. There were a few seconds of silence full of anticipation but, all of a sudden, the sound of my baby's heartbeat filled the room. It was music to my ears.

'Congratulations!' The sonographer turned to me. 'It looks like you're having a baby girl.'

# JORDAN

'Wow,' I exclaimed with a grin, staring at the black and white image on the screen. 'I can't believe it.' The idea of having a little mini-me felt like a dream. We can be like two peas in a pod, I mused to myself. My first thought upon learning that I was expecting a girl was that it was fate – it could be my opportunity to right the wrongs I had been dealt. But then the reality dawned on me and I started to panic. *I'm going to have to protect this girl from the whole world.* I knew all too well of the men out there who would wish her harm, and it would be my job to ensure that never happened to her. *I'm going to make sure this baby is raised right.*

Once home, I went straight round to Nan's to show her the picture, the pair of us debating on whether the baby looked like me or Blaine. For the rest of the pregnancy I spent as much time with my nana as I could, not wanting to be on my own. I had chosen Auntie Joanne, my mum's twin sister, to be my birth partner, but I also knew that I wanted Nan to be by my side every step of the way. One morning in September, the three of us made our way to the hospital so I could be induced.

'You're not going to have the baby today,' a nurse told us, as she helped me into a hospital bed, and she was right. I had periodic contractions all afternoon but it wasn't until the next day that I was moved into a delivery suite. I decided not to tell Blaine I was in labour. Deep down I knew it was wrong to keep it from him, but by then we weren't on speaking terms. I'll tell him when the baby's born, I thought.

# PIMPED

The contractions started to come more frequently and the pain was like nothing I had ever experienced. I tried to use the gas and air offered to me but it had started to make me feel sick, so I decided to give birth completely naturally. I was almost hysterical from the agony. Tears streamed down my face.

'It's time to push now, Sammy,' the midwife told me.

'I don't know if I can,' I admitted in a panic, but Auntie Joanne took hold of my hand and gave it a tight squeeze.

'Of course you can do this,' she reassured me, mopping my sweating forehead. It was the hottest day of the year and all I could think about was how warm the room was. I pushed as much as I could, sobbing in between the words of encouragement from everyone in the room.

After thirty-three hours of excruciating pain, I gave one final push and, for the first time, heard my baby's cries. Euphoria washed over me. I've done it, I thought. I can't believe I've done it. It was 4.26 p.m. on the dot, a time I could never forget, and I lay there in shock as the midwife presented me with my baby.

'He's got a willy,' I laughed, delirious from the pain. 'He's a boy!' The sonographer had got it wrong about the gender but my little boy was beautiful all the same. The midwife told me he was healthy, weighing 6lb 11oz, as his tiny face screwed into a frown as he wailed. He's perfection, I thought. Holding him for the first time was strange – as though all of sudden everything in my life had changed. I had heard people talk about the maternal instinct – that it just naturally takes over – but that was the one thing I had worried wouldn't happen for me.

The midwife placed him onto my chest and, like magic, he stopped crying. His big brown eyes looked into mine and it was like we had always known each other. Staring at his little face, I realised I was looking at something completely brand new, not yet marked by life's trials and tribulations. There was no trauma to keep him up at night, no pain in his eyes. He was fresh and clean, like a brand new slate, and he was perfect. Tiny flecks of green dotted about his dark eyes. Just like Blaine, I marvelled, unable to take my eyes off my newborn. I had never seen anything so beautiful in my life.

'Happy birthday, babes,' I whispered, tucking his fragile head safely under my chin. Up until this point my life had been a place of turmoil, entrenched in disorder and upset. But now time was standing still. Holding my baby close to my chest, I felt calm, as if nothing else mattered.

'His name is Jordan,' I mumbled to nobody in particular but I caught a glimpse of my nan smiling at me.

'That's a lovely name,' she cooed. I noticed the tears rolling down her cheeks and, suddenly, I wanted to cry. The room was full of love, like a safe bubble away from the world, and before long we were all crying, Nan, Jordan and I. We were a chorus of sobs and cuddles but it was amazing. I was so overwhelmed by the love I had for him but, at the same time, I had a niggling thought in the back of my mind: he's going into care tomorrow, I reminded myself. I shouldn't get attached. I had only known Jordan for ten minutes but I couldn't imagine life without him. Distraught, I passed him over to my nan. It's for the best, I tried to convince myself. I have to protect myself from getting hurt. I knew by then it was too late to keep him, and there was nothing I could do now to stop it from happening.

Within half an hour of giving birth, my support worker, Joy, arrived to meet Jordan.

'Oh, he's so gorgeous, Sammy,' she gushed, picking him up in her arms. I beamed proudly. I couldn't believe I had created something so perfect.

I was allowed to spend the first night in hospital with Jordan. The nurses trusted me to be unsupervised, so I woke up every three hours to feed him his bottles and change his nappies. I didn't sleep. Instead I cuddled my baby all night, scared to let him go in case someone came to take him away. The next morning the nurses praised me on how well I'd looked after him. If only I could look after him forever, I wished.

As morning turned into afternoon, family started to trickle in. First, my dad arrived, followed by my grandad and sister. The rule on the ward was that Jordan was allowed just two visitors at a time, but the midwives took pity on me. They knew Jordan was due to be taken into care.

'Let them all in,' one of the nurses told another at reception, so all of the family piled into the little room. Everyone got a cuddle with Jordan, in awe of how gorgeous my baby was.

'He's precious.' Dad beamed, wrapping me up in a warm hug.

'He is,' I agreed, not taking my eyes off him. Everyone was smiling and laughing, cooing in baby voices to the new arrival. All of them were there purely to say hello to Jordan – and, ultimately, goodbye.

It was late afternoon when two social workers arrived. A man and a woman walked into the hospital room carrying an infant's car seat. I sat on the bed staring at them as I held Jordan close to my heart.

'You've got ten minutes,' the woman told me. 'Then we need to go.' I glared at her. After experiencing the best day of my life, reality hit me like a ton of bricks. But Jordan is mine, I pleaded internally. He belongs with me. I couldn't bear the thought that someone was about to rip my baby away from me. I cried my eyes out, begging them not to take him.

'You'll have to tear him from me,' I choked out between desperate sobs. I cradled Jordan in my arms, not willing to give him up. 'I'm his mum.'

'Come on, Sammy,' Nan said, putting her arm protectively around me. 'You don't want to upset Jordan.' I looked down at the perfect doll-like baby in my arms. She was right. He was fast asleep, completely unaware that he was about to be uprooted from his family.

'Okay.' I lowered my voice, not wanting to disturb him. 'Let's get you ready.' Carrying Jordan carefully to the car seat was the hardest thing I had ever done. I wrapped him gently in a blanket, clipping his belt into place. I wiped away the tears that had dripped onto his face as I kissed him. 'There you go. You're nice and snug now.'

Jordan looked for all the world like an angel, perfect in every way. How am I supposed to go on without him? I wondered. I wanted to scream but instead I whispered softly to my baby. 'You're going home now, babes,' I cooed, my cheeks burning from crying. 'You're going home.' I just didn't have the heart to tell him he wasn't coming home with me.

# 15.

# DOWNWARD SPIRAL

**S**aying my goodbyes to Jordan was the most painful thing I had ever been forced to do. All too aware of my chaotic and unstable life, social services had given me two options: either sign Jordan willingly over to them and keep my parental rights or have him taken away on an order and lose any right I had to my little boy. What choice did I have? I couldn't bear the thought of losing Jordan entirely. I knew what I had to do and, with a heavy heart, I signed the paperwork.

Jordan was exactly one week old when I was allowed to see him again but it felt like it had been an eternity since I'd last gazed lovingly at my son. Jordan had been placed in temporary care with foster parents who I desperately wanted to hate but, meeting them for the first time at the contact centre, my heart sank. They're lovely, I realised, devastated to admit it, even to myself. *Jordan is so lucky to have them.* The couple beamed at me as they placed my baby carefully into my arms.

'He's grown already,' I exclaimed in shock. The social worker supervising the visit chuckled but I was deflated. I had been apart from him only one week and already I was missing out on things.

'Look.' Jordan's foster mum gestured towards him, sympathetically. 'He knows who you are.' Jordan was staring intently at me with a curious look on his face and I smiled. The afternoon I spent kissing and cuddling him went by in a flash. I couldn't wait to see my baby again and, after that, I went every weekday without fail to spend a couple of precious hours with him. I lived for the time I got to spend with Jordan at the contact centres. There I did everything I was missing out on, such as feeding him and changing his nappy. We had skin-to-skin contact and played together, and every day, as our visit came to an end, I welled up at the thought of saying goodbye again. I would go home alone to an empty house, unsure what to do.

Unable to cope with the guilt, I gradually started to depend on the drugs again. I hated myself for doing it, and at first I tried to convince myself there wasn't a problem. It's just a bit of weed, I thought, not wanting to think about it, and for a while weed was all it took to help me forget the mistakes I'd made. But soon I slipped into taking cocaine. I blamed Amanda for why I had lost Jordan. She made me this way, I seethed, in a drug-induced haze. *She's the reason*

*I'm like this.* I could feel my life tumbling drastically off the rails and there was nothing I could do to stop it.

Despite the drugs, I never missed a visit with Jordan, managing to force myself to be sober enough to see him. I knew I couldn't be a proper mum to him, not yet – I just wasn't stable enough. Being apart from my little boy was so painful that I tried to fight the bond I had with him. It won't hurt as much if I pretend not to care, I tried to convince myself, but every time I saw him I loved him even more than the last, and I treasured the time we got together.

'You're doing well with the visits, Samantha,' a social worker told me one day. 'If you keep it up we could be looking at having contact visits away from the centre and, at some point, even unsupervised visits.'

'Really?' I replied. I couldn't believe it. Even though everything else in my life was mayhem, every day felt like a step closer to getting Jordan back. Being at the contact centre five times a week meant I rarely strayed far from Grimsby but, as much as I avoided Sheffield if I could help it, I still made the odd trip to see my mum.

'Is everything okay?' she asked one day, noticing the look on my face as she opened the door. Mum's life had settled as the kids had got older but I still didn't want to burden her with the truth.

'Yeah, fine,' I lied. I couldn't tell her about the drugs I was taking or how desperately bare the cupboards in my house were. Catching up with Mum was always a nice break away from the norm, and seeing her in a more stable state than she had ever been before was comforting. It wasn't until I left her house that I fell back to reality. Have I ruined my life? I worried, wondering if I'd ever get Jordan back.

I was traipsing back through my old neighbourhood of Pitsmoor when I shuddered, remembering all the nearby houses that had hosted the dreaded parties. Bordering on panic, I was suddenly compelled to get out of there. Looking around, I noticed a family across the road. A middle-aged woman was pushing a double pram along the street with two toddlers in tow. A man had his arm around her. They looked like any other ordinary family, but looking carefully at the man's face I stopped dead in my tracks. I recognise that face, I thought, although at first I couldn't place him. He was Asian and, spotting the grey in his hair, I figured he must have been at least forty. He looked back at me standing on the other side of the road. I couldn't tell if he knew who I was but he immediately put his head down and carried on walking.

Suddenly it dawned on me – he had attended some of the early parties Amanda had taken me to when I was fourteen. My blood ran cold. I knew he had slept with Amanda. I felt weak. Wanting to get as far away as possible, I ran back to the train station, not daring to turn around. Once home I tore through the house in search of my secret stash. He has kids, I realised, horrified, as I found a tiny bag of cocaine in the kitchen. I'll never see him again, though, I told myself, trying to calm down. There's nothing I can do anyway. I sniffed a line of the white powder to forget what I had seen.

But the weed and cocaine weren't strong enough to fight the guilt that followed me around, and before long I decided to pay Pimps a visit. He was a dealer I'd seen around at parties in Grimsby. I never found out his real name but I knew he sold drugs from his house. Maybe he has something stronger for me, I thought, before heading over. I hesitated before knocking on his front door but, after a couple of minutes, Pimps answered, ushering me into the house.

'Have you got any gear?' I asked, following him into his living room. The room looked bare, with just a sofa and a coffee table facing the TV in the corner. Pimps was only in his thirties but his weathered face made him look a lot older. He was sporting a matching tracksuit and a cap to cover his overgrown hair.

'Yeah, sure,' he replied, disappearing into another room for a moment. I sat down on his couch, nervous that I may have been making a mistake. I'd never done anything as strong as heroin but, before I could change my mind, Pimps returned with a small bag of powder.

'I don't know what I'm doing,' I admitted, as he tried to pass the drugs over to me.

'You've never had it?' he asked, pausing. 'Are you sure you want to?' I knew he was just worried about getting into trouble if anything happened to me.

'Yeah, I'm sure,' I replied, and he agreed we would use it together. I perched myself on the edge of the sofa, my stomach doing flips as he showed me how to burn the powder on the tin foil before I breathed it in. I instantly fell back, sinking into the couch. I couldn't move. My entire body went limp and, forgetting about all of my worries, I felt like I was flying. This is amazing, I thought. *I want to feel like this all of the time.*

After that, I couldn't wait to try it again, but no matter how hooked I became on smack, I couldn't recreate that first high. Instead, it would paralyse me to the ground and, with a horrible pain spreading across my head, I felt like I'd be sick. But I couldn't stop, using heroin regularly before moving onto crack. It was as if, after losing Jordan, I had lost my mind. Good things don't happen to people like me, I thought bitterly. And the one good thing I had, I ruined. I hated myself for failing Jordan, and self-harm quickly became another way to punish myself for it. It evolved into being another one of my methods for self-destruction, and it wouldn't take much to trigger me. A nasty comment thrown my way and I'd flee to the solace of my home and cut myself.

My addiction was becoming increasingly expensive and, with no means to fund it, I felt like I had no other option but to start shoplifting again. At first it was just bits and pieces I could lift discreetly in shops. I tried to justify it by thinking it was nothing major, but at my lowest point I was sneaking into HMV and stealing at least 200 DVDs a day. I realised I could easily sell them on to second-hand shops and that became the way I paid for my habit. Any concern I used to have in previous years about getting caught had gone completely out of the window. I just didn't care anymore.

As Christmas approached, I felt sick at the sight of all

of the toys displayed in the shop windows. This will be Jordan's first Christmas, I thought to myself. And his first one without me. The idea of spending Christmas without my little boy didn't feel right. What was the point? He should be with me, I thought, crying on my own. Without Jordan there, all I wanted was for the day to pass with as little recognition as possible, but Nan wouldn't allow it.

'You're coming round for Christmas dinner,' she insisted down the phone.

'I don't want to–' I tried to refuse, but Nan wouldn't let it go and so, on Christmas Day, I begrudgingly made the short walk round the corner to my nan and grandad's house.

It was a quiet afternoon, listening to the pair of them chat about the soaps. I'll just get the dinner over with and then I can go home, I told myself, eager to forget the holiday altogether.

'I've got a surprise for you, Sam,' Nan announced, grinning. She got up from her seat at the table to fetch a wrapped present from under the Christmas tree. 'Here you go, open it.' She passed the box over to me.

'Thanks,' I muttered, instantly regretting my tone. I hadn't meant to sound ungrateful but presents were the last thing I wanted. I tore through the paper and was surprised to find a digital camera. I looked up at her, clutching the present in my hands.

'It's for your contact visits with Jordan,' Nan explained, glancing over at my grandad.

'We want you to have memories that you can look back

on,' he added, the pair of them smiling sympathetically at me. I felt the corners of my eyes prick with tears.

'Thank you,' I replied, and this time I meant it. It was as if they always knew exactly what to do to cheer me up.

Living near my nan gave me the stability I lacked from other members of my family, and I had been in Grimsby for a few months when David got in touch. I hadn't heard from my brother in a long time but I knew from passing rumours that he had been in and out of trouble with the law.

'Please, Sammy,' he begged me down the phone. 'I've got nowhere else to go.' David was on the run for burglary and needed a place to hide. While I still felt a sense of loyalty to my little brother, I knew if I got involved there was a high chance I could get in trouble. I paused before answering.

'I don't know,' I replied cautiously, as he continued to plead with me. I felt a pang of guilt. In the old days, David and I had been as thick as thieves and would have helped each other out no matter the consequences. 'Fine,' I agreed eventually, not wanting to let him down.

It was three days after Christmas when David arrived at my door, shivering and hungry.

'I haven't got anything for you,' I told him, searching through my empty cupboards, embarrassed to tell him how much I was struggling. I rarely ate apart from the occasional sausage roll from Greggs.

'We need to get some money,' David said, pacing around the living room.

'I know,' I agreed, shrugging my shoulders. Growing up,

stealing was all David and I had ever done together and it seemed to me like an easy way to scrape some cash. 'I could go get more DVDs,' I offered, but David shook his head.

'It's not enough. We need to make more than that,' he replied. 'This is a student area, right?' he added, and I nodded at him. There was a university nearby and a lot of students rented houses on my street.

'Why?' I asked, confused as to how this helped us.

'There will be students walking home from university tonight with laptops,' David explained, as I processed what he was suggesting. 'We could rob them.' I gulped.

'We might get caught,' I warned him, the whole plan making me feel uneasy.

'It'll be fine,' he flippantly reassured me. 'We need the money more than they do. It won't matter.' I knew what David was saying wasn't right, but I was too desperate to think rationally.

We waited until it was dark before heading out. I followed David along the street, listening to his footsteps as I tucked my hood low over my eyes. Suddenly he stopped and I looked up. There were two young girls on the other side of the road and one was carrying a messenger bag.

'I bet there's a laptop in there,' David whispered, pointing at the bag.

'Probably,' I replied, and David started to walk towards them. I trailed behind, my stomach doing flips as we approached. The plan recited by David was that he would talk to them as a decoy and I would pretend to have a knife.

I placed my hand behind my back so they couldn't see I was empty-handed.

'Eh up, girls,' David jeered, as he strode over to them. 'What's happening?' The girls looked about eighteen years old, with full make-up and push-up bras. This'll be easy, I told myself, in a bid to stay calm. Cornering them both near a wall, David lowered his voice.

'Hand everything over now,' he suddenly ordered in a menacing tone, grabbing one of them by the arm. I stood frozen, nearly as scared as the girls we were robbing. David glared at me and I jolted.

'Hand over everything or I'll stab you,' I chipped in. I moved the arm I was hiding slightly and one of the girls yelped. After a few pushes and cross words, we scared them into passing us the messenger bag. In a flash, we snatched it from them and ran away, leaving them crying on the street. Adrenaline got us home in record time, and by the time we made it back to my house I felt unstoppable. 'All of our problems are solved,' I laughed, placing the bag down on the kitchen table, ignoring the growing feeling of guilt in the back of my mind. But when I came to open it, I wanted to scream.

'Fuck!' I shouted, turning to David.

'What's wrong?' he asked, and his face fell when he saw. I pulled out the contents. We had just robbed two girls in the street and all we had to show for it was a pile of dirty washing, a tenner and a BlackBerry.

'What was the point?' I mumbled, pushing everything to the side. 'We could have been caught for that.'

'At least we weren't,' David answered, walking away to light up a cigarette in the front room before offering me a drag.

'That's true.' I sat down next to him. At least we got away with it, I thought, and for a couple of days it seemed like we had. But CCTV had picked up a tattoo on my hand and it didn't take long for police to catch up with us.

In the New Year I was arrested and brought into the police station for questioning.

'Take a look at this,' one of the officers said, playing back the footage from that night, and I cringed. Watching the footage, there was no denying David and I were the ones on the screen.

I was let out on bail but, because David had been wanted for burglary, he was remanded until our hearing in four months' time. I took it as a sign. I decided I needed to get clean before the court date, determined to sort my life out for Jordan. I restarted my regular visits with my support worker, Joy, and she helped me to stay out of trouble. It turned out that the girls we had mugged were far younger than we thought, and I knew I could be in a lot of trouble for it. I quit the drinking and the drugs and took up parenting courses in a bid to better myself.

'Where are we off to today?' Joy asked, turning up at my door.

'I need to go to the job centre,' I told her, and she smiled, then drove me to my appointment. Joy was a kind woman, in her thirties, with short black hair. Her refined accent led to me nicknaming her 'Posh Spice', and the pair of us always joked when we were together. I didn't go anywhere unless she was with me, too scared in case I got myself into more hot water.

'Do you think if I keep up this good streak that social services will let me have Jordan back?' I asked her one day.

'I don't know, Sammy,' she replied. 'But it's worth a go.' I knew that Joy was right and I threw everything into trying to be someone who deserved to have their baby with them. I became obsessed with baby clothes, hoarding them in the house and pretending Jordan was there to wear them. It was like I was missing a limb. As my court date approached, Joy took me to a meeting with my lawyer, and it was there that the reality of my situation became clear.

'I don't want to sugar-coat it,' he told me, looking through my notes. 'Taking everything into account, I think you're looking at about eight to twelve years.'

'In prison?' I asked in horror.

'Yes,' the lawyer confirmed, as I sat stunned into silence. 'You also need to know that if you get any longer than twelve months' jail time, the likelihood is that your son will be put up for adoption.'

'That can't be right . . .' I started to argue before trailing off. Jordan is going to be adopted, I thought, and felt sick. He's never going to know who I am. I had anticipated a sentence but I would never have expected it to be as long as eight years. I felt my stomach tie itself into anxious knots. I'll never get Jordan back now, I realised, and I burst into tears.

Giving up on any last hope I had, I spent the days leading up to the hearing selling off anything valuable I had left in the house. My PlayStation, stereo, any clothes I knew I couldn't wear in prison, they all had to go. If I don't get some money together for prison, I'll be stuck, I thought, remembering how life inside worked from my days at HMP New Hall. The night before I was due to appear in court, I threw a house party and everyone I knew in Grimsby turned up.

'Come in and trash my house,' I said, laughing, opening the door. I didn't recognise half of the people who turned up, but I didn't care. I wouldn't be seeing the light of day for a long time. Everyone brought drugs and booze with them, and when someone offered me M-Cat, I accepted, and soon everything became hazy.

The next morning, still in a drunken daze from the previous night's events, I made my way to Grimsby Crown Court. Outside the entrance, I waved as I spotted Joy and she ran over to give me a hug.

'I don't want you to come in,' I told her. I knew the outcome wasn't going to be good and there was no point in having a support worker now I was going to prison. She agreed and, after a tearful goodbye, I made my own way inside.

On 24 April 2013, at half nine on the dot, I took my place in the dock and held my breath. This is it, I thought to myself. I noticed Mum sitting in the public gallery and gave her a subtle nod. She's probably just worried about her golden boy, I thought, glancing at David, who was standing beside me. The pair of us stood in silence as the judge went over the details of the case. I listened anxiously, waiting for the inevitable as he called my name. I looked up.

'A twelve-year sentence is realistic in this case, Miss Owens, but I'm going to take into consideration that you've had a child so I'm going to knock it down to eight.' My heart pounded. Eight years was a long time without my baby. I panicked, but the judge continued: 'I'm also taking into consideration that you grew up as a child in need, so I'll bring it down to six and, given your guilty plea, I'll bring the sentence down to four.' Oh my God, I thought to myself, my hopes rising. *I might walk out of here today.* 'I have been informed by social services that if you get less than a twelve-month custodial sentence you have a chance of getting your son back.' I felt a small smile twitch at the corners of my mouth. 'But you have decided a life of crime is more important than your son.' My smile faded. 'After what you have done, you don't deserve to be a parent. I'm sentencing you to three years.'

'No,' I sobbed. 'I need my son.' I turned for one last glance at my mum before I was led into the holding cell. *This can't be happening.* After a few minutes, one of the officers came for me.

'You've got a place in Holloway,' he told me, gesturing for me to get up.

'Holloway?' I repeated, confused. 'But that's all the way in London.'

'That's the only place we've got for you right now,' he replied, but I shook my head, refusing to stand up.

'You can't send me to Holloway, I have a son,' I begged. 'I have visits with him.'

Luckily the staff at the court were understanding, calming me down as I cried. They spent the rest of the evening trying to find a prison closer to home while I sat alone in the holding cell. Given David's extensive criminal record, he had been handed a seven-year sentence, but even my three years felt like an eternity to me. At 10 p.m., an officer finally returned.

'There's a place for you in New Hall,' they announced, and I immediately stood up. I was heading back to the Wakefield prison I had been in when I was fifteen.

# 16.

# PRISON

What the judge had said to me in the courtroom really hit home: I just wasn't fit to be a mother. I sat in the back of the van for the duration of the trip to New Hall and sobbed. I could have easily got Jordan back, I thought bitterly. Just a few more months and he would have been with me again, but I ruined it. I couldn't believe it. Everything in my life had fallen to pieces and I knew that even if I got my act together now I'd be three years too late for my little boy. I'd failed him.

I was crouched with my head in my hands when I felt the van come to a stop. I looked up as an officer opened the door.

'Come on,' he said gruffly, and moved to the side slightly as I stepped out of the van. 'Let's go.' They escorted me into the prison, where I was met by a prison warden.

'We need to search you,' she informed me, and I followed her to be strip-searched. Afterwards they placed me in another holding cell, where I was handed an ID card. 'You must have this with you at all times,' the warden instructed, and I nodded, clipping it to my trousers.

The crime for which you'd been sentenced determined whether or not you would be sharing a room with another girl. Robbery was classed as a violent crime, so I was shown to an empty cell. Each wing of the prison was painted a different colour and my room was situated in what was dubbed 'the pink wing'. Resting against the baby-pink painted wall was a metal bed frame with a plastic mattress. I sat down. I guess this is my new home, I thought, subdued. Alone in the room, my mind wandered back to Amanda. I wonder what she's doing now, I thought to myself. Does she know I'm in prison?

Even though I had been sent to prison before, HMP was a world away from the young offenders unit and I was petrified. I arrived timid and shy, not wanting anyone to notice me, but, instantly, I became an easy target. For the first two months I sat back in silence, observing how the other girls acted around each other and accepting any bullying that came my way. We were woken up every morning at 7 a.m. by the blaring alarm that sounded around the prison. Hastily I'd jump out of bed to fold the sheets, making sure to be up, dressed and standing ready for inspection by half seven.

Selling most of my belongings before my court date

meant I went to prison with £300 in my account, which I used for the weekly shop order we were given. Buying more tobacco than I needed made me popular with the other girls, and I kept it up to make my life easier. I quickly learnt how to blend in and keep my head down in the hope I would get through the next three years with as little trouble as possible. I'm not going to be released as the same person who was sent away, I told myself, determined to make things right in my life. In a further bid to change my ways, I was even baptised into Christianity at the prison chapel and started to regularly attend the services they held.

For a while life plodded along, but apart from the occasional letter from Blaine, I hadn't heard from anyone on the outside. A few weeks after I arrived, one of the wardens came to my room.

'Owens, you have a visitor,' he said, after knocking on the door.

'Really?' I asked, surprised. *Who could it be?* Immediately I sprang to life and followed him down the corridor to the visitation room. I was so excited at the prospect of a visitor and it didn't take long to find out who it was. Amongst the small crowd of other people's loved ones, I spotted a tiny and familiar face, and I beamed. I sat down at a table as the social worker carrying Jordan made a beeline for me.

'Hi Sam,' she said, smiling, with a sleepy Jordan on her hip.

'Hey,' I replied, not taking my eyes off my gorgeous little boy. 'Can I hold him?' The social worker passed Jordan over to me and I cradled him in my arms. I didn't say anything, watching instead in awe as he started to doze off.

'How are you finding it here?' she asked after a few minutes.

'It's alright,' I answered, hesitating. I could sense there was something she was here to say. 'I've missed him.' The social worker gave Jordan a small smile before turning back to me with a serious look on her face.

'I'm sure you're aware by now that as you're in prison we need to start the process of adoption for Jordan.' She spoke slowly. 'We need you to sign over your parental rights for–'

'What if I refuse?' I interrupted, shaking my head in protest. I couldn't imagine willingly giving up my rights to my own baby. 'I'm his mum,' I added, protectively.

'You're entitled to refuse, Sam,' she replied softly, 'but the reality is that it will just prolong Jordan's stay in foster care until we get a court order. And we want to get Jordan to a permanent family as soon as possible.' I looked down at the precious baby asleep in my arms; he looked for all the world like Blaine.

'I can't do it,' I admitted, giving him a tighter squeeze. *How could I?*

I was given an hour to spend with Jordan but, after I left, I couldn't get the thought of his adoption out of my head. My mind raced back to my own upbringing of constantly moving in and out of children's homes. *I don't want Jordan to remember being in care,* I realised, knowing all too well what growing up as a care kid was like. *I want him to have a family that loves him.* I imagined Jordan with a stable home, with a mum and a dad who had cars and money to buy him nice things. Am I wrong to keep that from him? I wondered. I felt torn, the thought pricking my conscience every day until the social worker returned a few weeks later to plead the case. Even then, I was still at a loss for what to do.

'We have a lovely family lined up for Jordan,' she told me, explaining in detail the new life that was awaiting him. 'We'd love to give him a permanent home.' I sat across from her and listened in silence. Stop being selfish, I told myself. Let him go and be happy.

'But I won't get to see him again,' I blurted out, and suddenly I wanted to cry. Jordan was the only thing keeping me sane while I was locked up. I felt myself blush with embarrassment as tears rolled down my cheeks. I hated that she was seeing me upset.

'I know it's hard,' the social worker replied, offering me a tissue from her handbag. 'But sometimes we have to put our own feelings aside and do what's best for Jordan.' I felt a pang of guilt.

'I want to be a good mum,' I said. *But what if being a good mum means giving Jordan up?* I was trying harder than ever to make Jordan proud of me but, deep down, I knew what he needed me to do. 'I'll sign,' I muttered, unable to look her in the eye. I felt the weight of the world on my shoulders as she produced the documents and handed me a pen.

10 October 2013 was the date they gave me for Jordan's

final visit. He was due to be adopted in the next couple of months and that meant I wouldn't be allowed to see him again. On the surface, that morning was the same as any other. I awoke at 7 a.m. to get ready for inspection before heading down to the canteen for breakfast, but something about the way people were treating me was a telltale sign that today was very different. Everyone in the prison knew what was happening and was treading on eggshells around me, offering to let me jump the queue for food. Even the officers seemed to take pity, letting me wear contraband make-up and do my hair nicely for the inevitable photos. At my request I was led to the chapel, where social workers had arrived to supervise the visit. With my newfound faith I wanted the chance to take Jordan to church with me for the first and last time. At least that's one thing I can do with him, I thought, as I walked to the chapel alongside a warden.

Opening the door at the back of the church, I spotted one of the workers sat amongst a pile of toys on the floor, playing with a now crawling Jordan.

'Come over,' she said, motioning to me, and I headed towards my little boy, scooping him up into my arms. I couldn't believe how much he had changed.

'You've got so big,' I told him, smiling as I kissed the top of his head. Jordan was just over a year old now and he was hitting more milestones than I could keep up with. I lifted him up to eye level, his tiny fists grabbing clumps of my hair. You'll have no memory of me, I realised. His gorgeous brown eyes were still the most beautiful thing I had ever seen. You idiot, Sammy, I thought to myself. How could you let that go?

The visit at the back of the chapel lasted over four hours, with hundreds of pictures being taken of the pair of us by the prison staff. They provided us with paints and colours, and I helped Jordan as he scribbled away on the paper. The two of us played for hours, making memories together. After a while, Jane, the prison chaplain, arrived.

'Would you like us all to pray?' she asked, waiting for me to nod in agreement before reciting a prayer. We sat around in silence as she spoke and I watched Jordan gurgle away happily. Quietly, I asked God to look after him for me before soaking up the rest of the precious time I had. I completely zoned out, as if I had tunnel vision and was unable to see anyone else around me. It wasn't until a social worker tapped me on the shoulder that I noticed everyone in the room had stood up.

'Sam,' she prompted, looking at her watch before repeating herself. 'Sam.'

'I know,' I answered, realising it was time to leave.

'Do you want to say goodbye?' she asked. The social worker picked Jordan up off the floor and stood beside me. I took hold of his little hand as he gave me a toothy grin.

'Okay, this is it,' I said to him, my voice shaking as I spoke. 'Be good for your mum and dad.' I felt a lump rise in my throat and, lowering my voice, I whispered: 'I'm so sorry, I love you.'

I couldn't bear to watch them walk away with him, so I

gave Jordan one last kiss before I left the chapel with a prison warden. As I made my way down the corridor, wiping the tears away with my sleeve, I heard the social workers leave the chapel and head in the other direction. Don't look back, I told myself, but I couldn't help it. Turning around, I watched Jordan giggle as he was carried towards the prison entrance, and the sound of his laughter was the most amazing thing I had ever heard. I love you so much, I thought, as I watched him leave.

Without Jordan I had no idea how I was going to cope. Missing teatime completely, I threw myself onto my bed and sobbed. Drugs were an expensive but easily accessible commodity in prison and, with Jordan gone, I didn't know what else to do. I cried myself to sleep for days after the final visit, and every time I let him cross my mind I felt like I was going to collapse. A daily fix became what I relied on most to cope with the pain and, within a few months, I'd become hooked on Subutex, an opioid used to treat heroin addicts. I didn't need much – one hit in the morning was enough to help me get through the day. I'd scoop the powder under my fingernail and sniff it.

Each day after breakfast we were sent to our assigned jobs around the prison. Some of the girls supervised the gym while others took workshop classes or packed boxes. The job everyone really wanted was gardening, but that was difficult to get, being allocated only to girls considered low risk or who had been sentenced for a non-violent crime. During my time at New Hall, I was given a job at a call centre on site. Every day I turned up to ring people on our list, asking them to fill in a national survey. I loved the job and even started to look forward to it. I enjoyed the opportunity to talk to someone different, who didn't know I was a criminal, and for the brief time I was on the phone, I pretended I was just an ordinary person with a day job. The wardens gave us a time limit for each phone call but I rarely stuck to it, especially if the person I had rung was elderly. I would chat away to them for nearly an hour if I didn't get caught.

At lunchtime we'd be sent back to our rooms, where a sandwich and a packet of crisps would be waiting on the door hook. I'd scoff the food down quickly before the alarm would sound again and everyone made their way back to work. At the end of each day we'd head to the canteen for tea, rushing to get a spot in the queue before the nice options were gone. I didn't bother talking to any of the other girls in the canteen; you had to be quick if you wanted enough time to eat before we were sent back to our rooms for the evening.

In the room next door but one to mine was a girl named Leanne. She looked a similar age to me and was known around the wing for being a hairdresser. One evening I left my room and knocked on her door.

'Will you cut my hair?' I asked when Leanne answered.

'Yeah, sure,' she agreed, standing in the doorway. 'Do you have any tobacco?'

'Yeah,' I replied, searching for the bag in my pocket. 'I've just bought some more.' The call centre job earned me

£40 a week and that went a long way in prison, allowing me to buy up extra tobacco to use as payment for other things. I passed the tobacco over to her and she let me into the room. Leanne was pretty, with blonde hair and fake tan, and, as she cut my hair, the pair of us struck up a conversation. For the first time since I'd arrived, I thought I'd finally made a friend.

After that evening, Leanne and I spoke most days, gossiping about the various girls we knew in the prison. Living in the same wing, the pair of us hung out together, laughing and joking whenever we got a chance – it soon became an escape from prison life. Before long, I considered Leanne to be my best friend, telling her everything about Amanda's case. She was my shoulder to cry on and it finally felt like I had somebody in prison that I could trust. I couldn't risk looking weak in front of the other girls, so I kept my torment over losing Jordan to a minimum, only confiding in Leanne on my worst days.

'I don't think I can go on without him,' I cried to her as she listened.

'You'll be okay, Sammy,' she comforted me. 'You know it was for the best and he'll be loved no matter what.' I nodded reluctantly. Every day I would try to get through the entire day without thinking about him but it was impossible – I loved him more than anyone else in the world.

I had been in prison for eight months by the time Amanda's trial started. Paul Badger had kept in touch with me while he worked on the case, reaching out every now and then to let me know what was happening, and it was Paul who told me the trial dates.

'You'll be called as a witness,' he forewarned me on a visit to the prison.

'I know,' I replied, mulling over the prospect of facing Amanda again. 'I think I'm ready for it.'

'Good, and we'll be here to support you through it all.' Paul gave me a smile before adding, 'You're not on your own.'

That evening, I confided in some of the other girls on the wing about Amanda. They were aware that I had the trial coming up but they had no idea what had really happened.

'She pimped you out?' one of the girls asked in shock, and I gave a small nod. The group of us were sat outside Leanne's door as we chatted.

'Are you nervous of seeing her?' she continued, but I shook my head.

'No, I'm not scared of her,' I replied, wanting to appear tough. I couldn't help but notice one of the other girls nudge Leanne as I spoke.

'You have to tell her,' she whispered, glancing over at me, but Leanne seemed furious at the suggestion.

'Shut up now,' she snapped back. 'You don't know what you're talking about.'

'Tell me what?' I asked, and suddenly the room went silent. 'Come on, you have to tell me now.' I wasn't about to let this drop.

'It's nothing.' Leanne dismissed the question, glaring at the girl next to her, but that didn't stop her.

'No it's not,' the girl insisted. 'You have to tell her, Leanne, it's not right.'

'What's not right?' I persisted, starting to feel angry. 'If Leanne is keeping something from me then I want to know what it is now.'

'Well, you're probably going to hate me,' Leanne started, and I felt the hairs on the back of my neck prickle. 'It's just the reason I'm in here.'

'What?' I asked, and suddenly I realised I had never been told what Leanne had been sentenced for. 'What did you get sent down for?'

'I'm in here because I pimped out a girl,' she answered. 'Sorry I didn't tell you.' I froze in disbelief. *Did I hear that right?*

'You did what?' I started to raise my voice as my mind raced. *She's no better than Amanda!*

'You heard,' Leanne replied, bluntly, shrugging her shoulders.

'How old was she?' I quizzed, feeling my hand start to clench into a fist.

'Fourteen,' Leanne admitted, and I immediately saw red. Unable to stop myself, I leapt towards her, swinging my fists uncontrollably. A couple of the girls started to shout but I ignored them. After everything I'd been through, I was still spending time with someone who was just like Amanda. I couldn't believe it.

'You bitch!' I yelled as I hit her, regretting everything I had confided in her.

# PRISON

'Break it up now!' A warden intervened to stop the fight and the two of us were split up. Two wardens dragged us apart and we were ordered to follow them to separate offices, both of us shouting at each other as we left.

'You don't understand,' I protested to one of the wardens. 'She sold a girl for sex.' I explained what had happened and was sent to see the prison counsellor. There, I relayed everything about Amanda and Leanne, barely stopping for breath for fear of crying.

'Okay, Samantha.' The counsellor nodded understandingly. 'Leave this with me.'

Following the incident, Leanne was moved from the wing. I had no idea if she was even still in the same prison but I didn't see her again after that. Under the circumstances, the prison let me off for the fight but, as I headed back to my room that night, I felt broken. Is there anyone in the world I can trust? I thought to myself. I was starting to think that everyone was as evil as Amanda. The day of the trial was fast approaching. I need to focus on getting justice, I decided. I wasn't going to let Leanne distract me.

More determined than ever, I awoke on the morning of Amanda's trial and was taken into the holding cell where I'd been placed when I first arrived. A warden passed me a black suit.

'You can change into this here while we wait for the car to come around,' he said, before shutting the cell door. I got dressed and waited until the warden returned to escort me to the car. Climbing into the back seat, all the terrible memories came flooding back. Amanda's going to pay for what she's done, I told myself, hoping she'd be sentenced for a long time. I'm finally going to be rid of her forever.

# 17.

# THE TRIAL

'How are you, Sam?' a voice asked from the front of the car. Deep in thought, I slowly looked up and was surprised to see Paul Badger turning around in the driver's seat with a smile planted on his face. Instead of his usual police uniform, Paul was dressed smartly in a black suit.

'I'm fine,' I replied, briefly smiling back. Amidst the anxious feelings growing in the pit of my stomach, it was a relief to see a familiar face.

'Good,' Paul replied. 'Just remember to stay focused on giving as much detail as possible and you'll be absolutely fine.' I nodded as Claire, my prison officer, sat down in the passenger seat.

'Are you ready, Sam?' she asked, as the car began to drive away from the prison.

'I think so,' I answered, peering out of the window. *It's too late to back out now.*

'Good,' Claire reassured me. 'It's going to be okay.' I wanted to believe she was right and, for the rest of the journey from New Hall to the courthouse, I tried not to dwell on the day ahead of me, laughing as Paul cracked daft jokes.

'Shall we put some tunes on?' he asked, pressing buttons on the dashboard until the radio turned on. I sat back, watching the countryside whizz by. About an hour later we arrived at Sheffield Crown Court and Paul led me to the room I needed to wait in until the trial began. I paused for a moment, taking in my surroundings. This room was different from the usual cells I had become accustomed to. There were snacks laid out on a table and a flat screen TV hung from the wall.

'Wow,' I marvelled, walking around. My handcuffs had been removed and Paul and Claire had no problem with me wandering around freely. They weren't keeping constant tabs on me and it felt nice to be trusted for a change. As I got ready to leave the room, Paul noticed my trainers peeking out from under my smart trousers. He barked out a laugh and pointed them out to Claire.

'You can take the girl out of Sheffield but you can't take Sheffield out of the girl,' he joked.

'Shut up,' I replied, but I laughed too. Having Paul and Claire by my side made me feel so much more at ease.

'Don't worry, Sam,' Claire told me, as I was led up the stairs to the courtroom. 'All you can do is tell the truth so just be as honest as you possibly can.' Wordlessly I took her advice on board, stepping into the massive courtroom, but as I made my way past the judge's seat I noticed a white screen that would hide me from view.

'I don't want that there,' I announced, turning back to Paul. I knew that the screen would keep me from seeing Amanda and the last thing I wanted was to hide from her. 'I want to face her. And I want her to see me.'

'I'm sorry, Sam.' Paul shook his head, gesturing for me to take my seat. 'But you're going to have to leave it there.' I didn't move, annoyed that I wasn't allowed to see her. I want to look Amanda in the eye, I raged to myself. I want to see her face when I tell everyone what she did.

'But I don't need the screen,' I started to protest, but Paul was adamant.

'It has to stay,' he repeated and so, with no other choice, I begrudgingly took my place behind it. I felt stupid, but as I listened to the echo of people piling into the public gallery, I was grateful for the screen. I hope Mum isn't here, I thought to myself. She had wanted to come along but I wouldn't let her. Even though we hadn't always had a good relationship, I still couldn't bear the thought of her sitting through the details of what had happened to me. As Claire was my prison officer, she came to stand directly behind me, giving me a grin when I turned around to look at her. Everyone took their places, growing quiet as I heard Amanda being brought into the dock.

'Can you please state your name and address?' a lawyer asked me.

'Samantha Owens,' I answered, my voice shaking as I tried to calm my nerves. 'HMP New Hall.' Hearing my address, the room went silent and I blushed. Amanda's defence lawyer led the questions while I sat anxiously biting my nails.

'How are you?' he began.

'Fine,' I replied. This is going to be a waste of time, I thought to myself.

'Samantha, how did you meet Amanda Spencer?' he asked, and I described the first day I had spent with her at the markets. 'So, how did the two of you become friends?'

'From that day,' I told him, as I'd previously told Paul, 'we hung out and she took me to parties.'

'What parties?' he continued and I shrugged.

'Just parties,' I replied. Although I was hidden from sight, it felt like there were a thousand eyes on me, judging me for my past, and I was far too embarrassed to go into detail.

'Where were the parties?' the lawyer pressed on, wanting addresses from me, but I didn't want to offer any detail.

'Here, there and everywhere,' I said, rolling my eyes, trying to shrug the question off, hoping he would move on from discussing the parties. *Why can't we just focus on what Amanda did?* Every so often the questions would pause and the room would listen to the recording Paul Badger had made of my police interview. I silently cringed as the recording played out. *I wish I didn't have to be here for this bit.* I knew they needed it to compare my original statement with what I was saying now, but it was still painful to listen to. When the tape ended, Amanda's lawyer started to speak again, asking me how I had lost my virginity.

'It was at a party,' I told him, fidgeting uncomfortably in my seat.

'Who was it with?' he continued, not letting the subject go. 'What happened?' I took a deep breath, describing with as little detail as I possibly could the vile man who had raped me at thirteen years old.

'Was he rough with you?' the lawyer asked.

'Yes,' I stated.

'Why was he rough?' he quizzed, and I rolled my eyes. It felt like I was the one on trial instead of Amanda and, with every question he asked, I could feel myself getting more and more angry.

'I don't know, why don't you ask him?' I snapped back. I knew deep down it was his job to question me but I couldn't help but hear a slight judgement in his tone, like he didn't believe me.

'How do you feel about Amanda now?' the lawyer continued, not missing a beat.

'I feel abused,' I admitted, wondering if she was listening to anything I said.

'How do you know Amanda wasn't groomed herself?'

'Because she was the one who was always in control,' I countered, my voice rising. I didn't know how much more I could take of this. I feel like I'm being treated like a criminal, I thought to myself. I know I'm in prison but I'm a victim in this case.

'But is there not a chance she was also groomed?' the lawyer repeated again. They're acting like it was my fault, I thought, seething. Like I'd asked for it. I couldn't cope with the questions anymore.

'I need a break,' I said, turning to look at the judge, who was sat diagonally behind me. 'I need a break now.' The judge agreed and Amanda was taken back into her cell so I could leave the courtroom.

'You're doing great,' Claire told me calmly as I was led back downstairs. 'Just don't hold back.' I sat in silence, listening to her advice.

'Claire's right,' Paul added, joining us in the room. 'Don't be afraid to tell them everything.' I sat thinking. The lawyer had brought up the parties to discredit me, I realised, annoyed at how little we had discussed Amanda. I needed to make this about her.

After a short break, I returned to the courtroom ready to face another round of questions.

'You asked me how I know Amanda wasn't groomed,' I started to explain. 'I know because Amanda used the girls she was friends with; she was always in control.' I paused, thinking for a second that I had heard someone laugh, but I brushed it off. 'We were used to her advantage for sex, drugs and money.' Suddenly I was interrupted by a loud laugh. Who the fuck is laughing at me? I thought, unable to see what was happening from behind the screen. I tried my best to carry on and ignore it.

'She knew what she was doing,' I continued. 'She preyed

on vulnerable girls who were care kids.' The laugh broke out harder and I realised where it was coming from – *Amanda*. It was as if she was deliberately trying to be loud. She's showing off, I thought, and my blood boiled. It's her fault this happened to me and she still finds it funny.

'I was used by her–' I started to say but Amanda let out another cackle and, before I could rationalise my thoughts, I snapped.

'She's a fucking slag,' I shouted, letting the anger get the better of me. I jumped out of my seat, peering over the screen to look Amanda dead in the eye. We made eye contact and immediately she fell silent.

'Samantha, you need to sit back down,' the judge ordered but I wasn't paying attention; instead I didn't let Amanda out of my sight.

'You're a slag,' I shouted to her, determined to wipe the smug smile from her face. I hadn't seen her in years but she looked exactly the same. She had a big quiff of hair gathered at the top of her head with her ponytail tied to the side. She looked ridiculous, and I sniggered to myself.

'Samantha, if you don't calm down then you won't be giving evidence,' the judge warned and, giving Amanda one last glare, I fell back into my seat.

'I'm a victim too,' Amanda started to whine before the judge silenced her. I wanted to hit her but instead I rolled my eyes in horror. Amanda had never been made to do the things I had, I thought to myself. It was her who was the ringleader. I shook my head in disbelief, remembering the times she had instructed me on which house to go to or which man to follow to a bedroom. Amanda wasn't a victim, she was my abuser, but here she was finding my pain funny. Unable to cope any longer, I looked up helplessly at the judge.

'She's had enough,' he announced, coming to my rescue. The trial finished early for the day, as he sent everyone home and I followed Claire back downstairs. Watching her close the door behind us, I burst into tears.

'I hate her,' I shouted, unable to get Amanda's evil laugh out of my head. 'She has no remorse for what she's done.' I sat back in the holding room, curling my legs up to my chest, and waited for Paul Badger to arrive.

'How are you feeling?' he asked once he saw me, my face burning from the upset.

'I don't know,' I admitted, getting up to pace back and forth around the room, thinking, Have I made a mistake? I wished I'd offered more information when I'd had the chance. After a few minutes of silence, an idea came to me.

'I need to give my evidence again,' I thought out loud, realising my minimal detail could never be enough to send Amanda down.

'Are you sure?' Paul asked and I nodded.

'Yes,' I confirmed, determined to make sure I got justice. 'I have more I want to say.'

'Okay,' Paul replied, immediately agreeing. 'I'll sort it.' And with that, he left the room. I waited around with Claire until Paul returned to take me back to prison.

'You can give a new statement tomorrow,' he told me and I smiled.

'Good,' I answered, following them back to the car. That night I lay awake in my cell, mulling over the day's events. Amanda can laugh at me all she wants, I thought, staring up at the ceiling. But I'm going to make sure she pays for what she's done.

The next day I walked into the courtroom with my head held high, taking my seat behind the screen.

'Good luck,' Paul told me quietly before leaving me on my own. I glanced over at Claire before turning back around. I could feel my heart pounding in my chest as everyone started to arrive. You're determined, I told myself over and over again. *You can do this.* I listened as the same defence lawyer as the previous day started to question me and, this time, I wasn't going to hold back.

'Why do you want to change your statement?' he quizzed.

'Because I didn't go into detail yesterday,' I replied. 'And I didn't want to but now I'm ready to talk about it.'

'Can you talk to me then about the party where you lost your virginity?' he asked, and I hesitated, taking a deep breath.

'The first house was on Godric Road. I only knew to go there because Amanda had led me,' I told him.

'Was it her idea to go to the house?'

'Yes,' I answered. 'I didn't want to go but she was older than me and she pressured me into it.'

'What happened when you got there?'

'I was raped,' I replied bluntly. For a second, I clammed up, not wanting to discuss that night in court, but Paul's advice about giving as much detail as possible flashed into my mind. I needed to do this to stop Amanda.

'The man who raped me had a scar on his back,' I blurted out. 'It looked like a small cross on his shoulder blade.' I paused to think before adding: 'And I went to parties on Infirmary Road.' The address had sprung to mind as I spoke and, before I knew it, I couldn't stop talking, offering any piece of information I could think of that would help place Amanda at the scene.

'What did the sex with the men feel like?' the lawyer asked me. 'Were you forced or pinned against your will?'

'I wasn't physically,' I answered. 'But mentally, yes.'

'What do you mean?' he probed. 'How can you be held mentally if it wasn't physically?'

'I couldn't say no,' I replied confidently. 'I didn't have a choice.' I felt tears starting to prick the corners of my eyes but I didn't want to hold back anymore. I couldn't tell whether I was crying out of embarrassment or if it was that, for the first time, I was accepting that I didn't deserve what had happened to me. *Why was Amanda allowed to put me through that? I'm not going to let her get away with it.*

By the end of the day I was exhausted, falling asleep in the back of Paul's car as we drove back to New Hall.

'You should be proud,' he said, and smiled before Claire escorted me inside. 'You've done so well.' I headed back to my room in the pink wing and for a moment everything seemed surreal. Did all of that really just happen? I wondered, in disbelief that I had spoken out at a trial against Amanda.

For the next few weeks I carried on with normal life in the prison, spending my days at the call centre, avoiding any conversation in the canteen, but I couldn't get the trial out of my mind. I wondered if it was finished yet, although I was sure Paul would get in touch if it was. On the prison's advice, I started attending regular counselling sessions to help me with my trauma and it was my counsellor who called me into the office one day for a chat.

'Just to let you know, Amanda was sentenced today,' she told me, and immediately my ears pricked up.

'Well?' I asked, impatiently.

'She was found guilty on sixteen counts of child prostitution,' she revealed, as I held my breath, desperate to know the outcome. 'She's been sentenced to twelve years.'

'Yes!' I exclaimed, punching the air. 'I can't believe it.' On the one hand, I would have liked to see her get life behind bars but I was still happy, relieved that someone had finally listened to me and had taken me seriously. Old Man John had died awaiting trial but four other men stood trial for their involvement in the sex ring and, while three were acquitted, Ian Foster was jailed for fourteen years. He was found guilty of twelve sex offences against children. I left the counsellor's office feeling ecstatic. They believed me, I noted, having been let down so many times before. It was as though a weight had been lifted from my shoulders. Free from Amanda, I was ready to start my life again.

# 18.

# SERVING MY TIME

The days that went by after Amanda's conviction seemed to last forever. I had spent so much of my time with the looming responsibility of giving evidence weighing over me that now I didn't know how to pass the time. What am I supposed to do? I thought to myself. It was as if the trial had provided me with a purpose that pushed me through each day, but now I was trapped in a daze. I still had eighteen months left to serve and, at a loss, I continued to rely on my daily dose of Subutex. Entirely dependent on the opioid as I was, the next few weeks went by in a mundane blur, each week as meaningless as the last. Then one day, out of the blue, something changed.

'Owens!' One of the prison wardens flagged me down during free time. 'You've got some post.' The warden gave me a slight smile before walking away.

'Wow,' I muttered to myself, rooted to the spot in the corridor. 'But I never get any post.' *Who could have possibly written to me?* Curious, I ran straight back to my room. There I found an envelope waiting for me and, sitting down on my bed, I tore open the letter, but upon seeing the name signed at the bottom of the page, I fell to a stop. I can't believe it, I thought, in total shock. After months without any contact, Blaine had written to me for the first time. Overwhelmed, I started to read his note, the sick feeling in my stomach growing the more I read. When I had given Jordan up for adoption the previous year, Blaine had had no idea and, when he found out, he was heartbroken. Blaine wrote about what his life had been like for the past few months, that while I had been in prison, getting ready to face Amanda, he had been fighting for custody of our son. *I did everything I could to get him back,* I read. There was no father listed on Jordan's birth certificate and that meant Blaine needed a DNA test to prove he was Jordan's dad. I sat in disbelief, reading how, because of the number of men who were abusing me, social services had refused to pay for Blaine's test but, unbelievably, Blaine had managed to scrape together the £500 himself. Within a week of a DNA test confirming Jordan was his son, Blaine had full custody of our little boy.

'Jordan is living with Blaine,' I said out loud, astounded that the boy I had waved goodbye to was suddenly closer than ever. At first, my instant reaction was anger. How could Blaine do this? I seethed. Jordan had a chance at normal family life. My own life was in such disarray that I couldn't see a future for Jordan that would benefit from having me in it. But even still, I couldn't ignore the joy bursting in my chest at the thought of my little boy being within arm's reach. I'd thought I'd never hear about Jordan again, and just to know he was happy and healthy was the greatest comfort I could have ever asked for.

I concealed the letter in my room for safe keeping and, after the first one, Blaine wrote to me every single week. He told me all about Jordan, keeping me up to date with each milestone that passed as he grew older. Sometimes Blaine would even include pictures of Jordan, which I hung up in my room, marvelling at how much he had changed. We didn't speak over the phone, and Blaine never came to visit me; instead I had just a small reminder each week of life going on outside prison.

I carried on with the day-to-day schedule of life inside, waking up at seven in the morning to the blaring sound of the alarm. Reluctantly I would drag myself out of bed, barely eating any breakfast before heading to the call centre. I was still using Subutex to get me through the day. It's not like I'm taking a lot, I tried to convince myself, as I sat in the toilets. I scooped up a fingernail of the crushed tablet before putting it to my nose. I flushed the toilet loudly and, getting up, I headed back to work. I couldn't cope with the monotonous routine of prison life anymore.

'If you have five minutes to do a quick national survey–' I started before I was cut off mid-spiel.

'No, fuck off!' the other person shouted before hanging up the phone. I sighed, punching in the numbers for the next caller. It's never-ending, I moaned to myself. My only escape from prison was the weekly updates I got from Blaine. Reading for just a moment about how Jordan was doing made me feel that I was somehow still a part of his life, and that gave me hope. On Mother's Day I received a card signed from my little boy and I broke down into tears. This was a dream come true, I cried to myself. That day, many of the other mums walked around the prison carrying cards and gifts from their family. I smiled, treasuring the small card in my hand. For the first time I truly felt like a mother and, as the months went on, the maternal bond I'd immediately felt at Jordan's birth came flooding back. Blaine was the only person in my life to stick by me – and knowing that I at least had him to talk to gave me strength.

Desperate to see my little boy, I kept my head down, not involving myself in anything that could get me into trouble. Jordan needs his mum, I told myself. Determined to get out of prison as soon as possible, I isolated myself and, with no friends to spend time with, I ate alone every night.

'I need to get clean,' I thought to myself one night as I lay wide awake in my room. The date for my release was drawing closer and I was too preoccupied to sleep. I can't be an addict if I want to be a mum, I thought. I have to quit for Jordan's sake. I decided that I would ease myself off the drugs slowly and, at first, I tried hard to cut down. You don't need it, I tried to convince myself, whenever I felt the urge to use. I willed myself not to cave, thinking about how disappointed Jordan would be in me, but the lure of getting high only ever drew me back in.

After a week of trying and failing to give up my addiction, I knew there was only one way to do it – I had to go cold turkey. I was determined not to let Jordan down a second time. The minute the thought crossed my mind, I put it into action and, just like that, I had quit Subutex. I knew it wasn't going to be easy. It was something I had to force myself to stick to and, within a day, I had started to get the sweats. I couldn't sleep or eat, shaking as I crawled through the prison's daily routine. Whenever I had free time I lay bed-bound in my room, shivering uncontrollably from withdrawal. Can I even do this? I wondered in agony, but I wasn't ready to give up just yet.

For my last few weeks of working at the call centre, I barely made any calls. Instead I sat at my desk in a daze, my fingernails digging into my skin as I willed myself not to run out of the room. Turning my back on drugs was one of the hardest things I had ever had to do, but the family life Blaine was offering me was more than worth it.

The more days that went by, the easier it became to stay clean. My urge to use the drug was starting to subside, and one day I woke up and realised I wasn't shaking at all. My release date was imminent and, in preparation, I attended meetings with support workers who were helping me to prepare for life outside of prison.

# PIMPED

'First of all, we need to find you somewhere to live,' said one of the support workers organising my departure.

'I already know where I want to live,' I told her with conviction. 'I need to be placed in Chesterfield.'

'Are you sure?' they asked me, but I was adamant.

'Yes,' I insisted. 'Please don't place me anywhere else.' I was desperate to be close to my little boy.

'You have family in Grimsby,' one of them pointed out, but I shook my head.

'I've got bad ties in both Grimsby and Sheffield,' I explained, determined to steer clear of my past. 'I need a fresh start.'

'Okay.' One worker finally nodded in agreement. 'Let's make sure you get that fresh start.' They let me look through different flats in Chesterfield, allowing me to pick out the home I would move into. I looked carefully over my options and, spotting one particular flat, I became adamant that I needed to live there.

'It's perfect,' I told them and they agreed. Unbeknownst to anyone at the prison, the flat I was set on was just two streets away from Blaine's new house. The closer the better, I thought to myself. I knew if social services found out they wouldn't allow it, so I kept quiet about Blaine. They would prefer me to have supervised visitation but I couldn't wait any longer – I had already missed out on so much time. The letters from Blaine had given me a glimpse of what the future could look like for me, and I wasn't going to turn my back on it now. I was ready for my future to begin.

# SERVING MY TIME

On the day of my release, I awoke fresh-faced and clean from drugs. It felt amazing. I got myself ready and followed a warden to an office where he handed me a bag containing the few possessions I had come to prison with. I walked out of the double doors, the weight of the last three years falling from my shoulders. It was 8 a.m. and immediately the smell of morning dew hit me. *This is it. Freedom.* Once outside the prison I was met by a support worker I had never seen before.

'Hi Sam,' she said with a grin. 'I'm here to collect you if you're ready to go.' I'm more than ready, I said to myself, climbing into the passenger seat of her car. Once the prison was out of sight I breathed a sigh of relief, and the further away from Wakefield we drove, the more relaxed I felt. We're getting close to Chesterfield now, I thought, watching the road signs fly past on the motorway. Nearer to Jordan and Blaine. Unable to hide my emotion, I beamed as I sat staring out of the window, almost giddy with excitement. Each mile that passed felt like a leap towards the dream family I longed for.

# 19.

# A NEW BEGINNING

**U**pon arrival at my brand-new flat, I wandered around each room in awe. I smiled and took a deep breath with the realisation that it was all mine. My new life.

'What do you think?' my support worker asked me, raising her eyebrows before catching my grin. 'Will it do?'

'Definitely,' I gushed, jumping onto the sofa. 'I love it.' The flat itself was small, with just the basic amenities. It was furnished plainly with old tables and chairs but that didn't matter. For most of my time in prison I had thought there was no hope for the future, but this tiny flat was my starting point, and for that I was so grateful to be there.

'There's a few things we still need to get,' my support worker added, pointing out there was a kettle missing from the kitchen. 'But we can go shopping now for some bits and pieces if you'd like to.'

'That would be great,' I replied, excited, and with that we

headed back to the car. She drove us into Chesterfield town centre and, once there, the pair of us set off down the high street. There were plenty of things I didn't have – cutlery, bedding, pots and pans – but whatever I needed, my support worker bought for me. By the time we returned to the flat, both of us had our arms full with shopping bags. I plugged my new kettle into the wall to make us a brew before helping to set up the TV.

'I think you're all set,' she eventually announced, stepping back to marvel at the appliances we had assembled. 'I'll let you get on with your day.' She got up to leave and I followed her to the front door.

'Thanks for your help,' I said, smiling. I had no idea how I would have set up the flat without her.

'Not at all.' She grinned. 'Enjoy your life now, Sammy.' I waved her goodbye, shutting the door as she went, her words of advice ringing in my ears. *I will do.*

I spent that afternoon alone in the flat, enjoying my new surroundings as I cooked dinner. Home sweet home, I chuckled to myself, still in disbelief that this place was all mine. I loved it there already but, as the street outside darkened, my thoughts turned to my family just two streets away. Would it be too soon to get in touch? I wondered, glancing at my phone. Maybe a quick phone call wouldn't hurt. But I brushed off the idea, telling myself I should probably leave it a few days. I knew the sensible thing would be to wait but, before I could stop myself, I had picked up the phone and was dialling a familiar number.

# A NEW BEGINNING

'Hello?' I listened as Blaine answered the call and a smile spread across my face. His voice hasn't changed a bit, I realised.

'Hi, it's Sam,' I replied. 'I've just moved into my flat.'

'Oh hiya,' Blaine responded. 'What's up?' I hesitated, suddenly not knowing what to say. I racked my brains to think of an excuse for why I was calling.

'I was just wondering if you've got a DigiBox,' I said, cringing as soon as the question left my mouth.

'Yeah, I've got a spare one,' he answered before adding, 'Do you need it?' I stared at my own DigiBox placed under the new TV.

'Yes, I haven't got one,' I fibbed, needing an excuse to see him.

'Pop round if you want to,' he offered. We agreed I would wait until Jordan had gone to bed before I made my way round to Blaine's house at 8 p.m. It's the right thing to do, I thought to myself, even though I was desperate to see my little boy again. I knew I couldn't meet Jordan properly straight away; that would take months of building up to. I was nervous even of seeing Blaine again. It had been years since the two of us had spoken in person, but I needn't have worried.

'Hey!' Blaine exclaimed as he answered the door, throwing his arms around me. 'It's so good to see you,' he enthused, inviting me inside. 'Are you having a brew?'

I nodded, following him into the kitchen, and, within five minutes, it was like we had never been apart. The pair of us spent what felt like hours laughing and chatting, catching up on three years of life.

'You must be so relieved to be out,' he said, settling down in the living room. I grinned.

'You couldn't imagine how happy I am,' I answered him, almost laughing with happiness. 'I've got my life back.'

Blaine and I reminisced about old times, joking about the daft things we did as teenagers, and, after a while, I excused myself to head to the bathroom. For the two minutes I had alone, I couldn't stop smiling. Blaine is exactly the same, I thought, looking at myself in the mirror above the sink.

I took that rare moment of calm to reflect on the day's events. I can't believe this is my life, I thought. I'm so lucky. I left the bathroom and was heading back towards the stairs when I noticed a door decorated with stickers – Jordan's room. For a second I didn't know what to do, and was frozen to the spot on the landing. There's no chance of him being awake at this time, I thought to myself, hesitating as my foot hovered over the top stair. I took all of one step forwards before I changed my mind and turned back towards Jordan's room.

Slowly, I opened his door, being careful to be quiet. There he was, lying sound asleep in his bed. Oh my God, I marvelled. *He's so adorable!* Not wanting to wake him, I stayed by the door and watched Jordan as he dreamed. He's so grown up, I noted, with a tinge of sadness. The little boy I had said my goodbyes to in the chapel had been a baby, but now Jordan was three years old. I've missed him so much, I realised with a heavy heart. For a few minutes I stayed by his door, not wanting to take my eyes off his beautiful face. I knew it would be a long time before I'd get to meet him face to face and, while that reality stung, snatching a glimpse of him sleeping, even just for those few moments, was what kept me going. I went home that night with a full heart, excited for what the future held for me.

'Say hi to Sammy,' Blaine said, pointing to my picture on the phone screen, and Jordan waved shyly to the camera.

'Hello sunshine!' I beamed. It had been three weeks since I'd gone round to Blaine's house and the pair of us had agreed that speaking to Jordan on FaceTime for the first couple of months was a good way for him to get to know me. I don't want to force it, I thought, pulling faces at the camera. I want him to bond with me naturally.

'Sammy's silly,' Jordan giggled and I smiled. His laugh was the best thing I had ever heard.

When I wasn't talking to Jordan on FaceTime, I kept myself busy, organising my flat and focusing on staying clean from drugs. I'm not going back to that lifestyle, I reminded myself whenever temptation grew. Every now and again a support worker would arrive to check in on me and make sure I was okay, and each time they praised me on how well I was doing.

'You should be so proud of yourself,' one worker enthused. 'You're really making a go of it.' Hearing her praises of approval felt like recognition of the changes I had made to my life, and that felt amazing.

Over time, Blaine decided that Jordan was ready to meet me. It had been a couple of months in the making, building up the contact between us, but when he finally suggested it was time to see him, I was over the moon.

'Why don't you come round at lunchtime?' Blaine offered one weekend. 'So that you can spend a couple of hours with him.' I wanted to cry with joy.

'Absolutely,' I agreed, ecstatic at the news. 'I'll be round soon.' Eager to see my little boy, I quickly got myself ready before heading over to Blaine's house at the agreed time of noon. I knocked on the door, and suddenly a rush of nerves hit and my stomach tied itself in knots. What if Jordan hates me? I panicked, almost wanting to back out. What if he doesn't want me to be his mum? I couldn't think of anything worse, but I didn't have time to stress. Before I knew it, Blaine opened the door and, giving me a warm hug, he ushered me inside.

Jittery, I walked into the living room and there was Jordan, sat on the carpeted floor playing contently with his model cars. He's even cuter than I remember, I thought, as I made my way into the room. Noticing me, Jordan looked up, staring intently as I slowly moved towards him.

'Hello.' I grinned, crouching down beside him. 'I'm Sammy.'

'Hi.' Jordan smiled shyly, his hands covering most of his face.

'What are you playing?' I asked, trying not to fidget with anxiety. Blaine followed me into the living room and, spotting him, Jordan ran into his arms.

# A NEW BEGINNING

'Come on, Jordan,' Blaine said, and led him back to his toys. 'You're not shy.' I gave him space, sitting myself down on the sofa as Jordan returned to his games. I didn't want to seem disheartened but a small part of me wondered if he would ever think of me in the same way he thought of Blaine.

'I'll make us a brew.' Blaine excused himself, leaving the two of us alone in the living room. Too nervous to think of conversation, I fell silent. Instead, I watched Jordan run around the room, keeping me in the corner of his eye at all times. The room was hot and, anxious, I could feel myself sweating.

'Do you want to play cars?' he eventually said, pointing towards his toys, and my heart swelled.

'I'd love to,' I answered warmly, joining Jordan on the rug. He handed me one of his model cars.

'This one can be yours,' he told me before turning back to the others scattered over the carpet.

'Brilliant.' I smiled. Blaine returned to the living room and beamed at me, setting my cup of tea down on the coffee table.

'You two look like you're getting along,' he said, sitting down on the sofa. While Jordan and I played, Blaine sat back, allowing us to bond.

'I'm overtaking you,' I teased, running the car along imaginary tracks.

'No you're not,' Jordan giggled and I smiled. I don't think he understood exactly who I was but, as the afternoon wore on, Jordan seemed to warm to me. I let my tea go cold and the two of us played together for what felt like hours with Blaine laughing along with us from the sofa.

'I think that went well,' Blaine reassured me as I got up to leave.

'Do you think so?' I asked, and he nodded. I had been so worried about meeting my boy again, but being Jordan's mother was the most natural thing in the world. That night, as I walked home alone, I couldn't get the day's events out of my mind. Jordan has changed so much, I thought. But his eyes are exactly the same. I had forgotten how Jordan's eyes were the perfect mixture of mine and Blaine's, dark brown with glints of green that flickered in the sunlight.

After our first meeting I couldn't wait to see my little boy again, desperate to make up for the years lost, but the more time we spent together the more apparent it became that there was so much missing between us. Jordan had his own experiences and a big personality completely separate from me. I didn't recognise his mannerisms, and it hurt to realise that I didn't know my own son, but I was determined to get to know him. *I've lost so much time already. I'm not going to give up now.*

'Now, Jordan, it's up to you,' Blaine said, sitting him down on the sofa one afternoon. 'You can keep calling Sammy just Sammy, or you can call her Mummy.' At first, Jordan chose to keep calling me Sammy. That's perfect, I thought, not letting myself get upset. I could hardly expect to simply waltz back into his life after three years and act like his mum. I knew integrating myself with Jordan would take time and, after a few meetings, Blaine decided it was time to explain to him properly that I was his mum.

'Come and have a seat here.' Blaine gestured at Jordan to sit down on the sofa and, once he was paying attention, Blaine told him about how he and I had met.

'She had to go away for a while,' he explained to a confused Jordan, who scrunched his face up as he listened. 'But she's back now.'

'Okay,' he replied, and at first he seemed to accept Blaine's reasoning. He got up and went back to his toys, but after a little while he turned his attention back to me.

'Sammy,' Jordan started to say, his big beautiful eyes peering up at me.

'Yes, darling,' I answered, giving him a grin. 'What's up?'

'Where were you?' he asked. The question caught me off guard.

'Um...' I paused, not knowing what to say. 'What do you mean?'

'Where were you?' Jordan repeated. 'Before?' I fell silent and, for a moment, I wasn't sure how to respond. Do I tell him the truth? I wondered, looking over to Blaine for help.

'You can tell him if you want to,' he reassured me. I did want to. I needed to tell Jordan the truth, not wanting to have secrets from him. I was aiming to be as transparent about my past as I could with a three-year-old, knowing it could serve as a life lesson for him in the future. Choosing my words carefully, I answered his question.

'I was naughty,' I admitted, explaining it in a way he could understand. 'So I had to go to prison for a while.' Jordan was quiet and I sat in silence, letting him process what I had just told him. Finally, he looked up at me to speak.

'Are you a good guy now or a bad guy?' he asked and I couldn't contain my smile.

'I'm a good guy,' I replied, scooping him up in my arms. I planted a big kiss on his cheek before he wriggled free, laughing until I gave in and put him back down. I thought back to the version of myself that had been sent to New Hall. I couldn't even imagine turning back to the parties and the drugs now. It was like every day I got to spend with Jordan was healing me and I was an entirely different person to the one who had been sucked in by Amanda.

Over time, Jordan got used to having me around the house and began to call me 'Sammy Mummy', which he soon shortened to simply 'Mummy'. Blaine and I picked up from where we had left off and, before long, I was spending every day at Blaine's house. Hearing Jordan shout 'Mummy' in excitement every time I walked through the door made my heart burst with joy, and it felt like confirmation of how far we had come since our first FaceTime chat. Everyday life seemed to tick along smoothly until social services found out I was back in contact with Jordan. I was immediately called in for a meeting, and I was terrified of what was going to happen.

'You know we're not happy about this, Samantha,' one social worker informed me as he went through my paperwork. 'You should have gone through the proper channels.' Reluctantly I nodded in agreement.

# A NEW BEGINNING

'I know I should have,' I replied, ready to admit my faults. 'But I just couldn't wait to see him.' The separation from Jordan in prison had been torture enough. 'I've already missed out on three years,' I added quietly. I was petrified they would take Jordan away from me again. I can't lose him a second time, I thought, panicking to myself, but after several meetings with social services and one house visit, they decided that I was stable enough for regular contact.

'It's done now,' a social worker said to me during one of my meetings. 'We're not going to halt your contact now that you're already seeing him daily. As long as it's going well and Jordan's happy, I don't see any reason to stop it.' I was so elated I felt I was walking on air. With the social services' seal of approval, I was finally a proper mum to Jordan.

After that, there was no stopping us. With Jordan content to have me around, I moved into Blaine's house and, for the first time ever, our family was complete. There was still so much missing between me and Jordan, so many of his firsts that I had missed out on and, for a while, I dwelt on that. It felt as though nothing I did could ever make up for not being there from the beginning. As time went on, though, we learnt to create our own milestones.

'You know,' I commented to Blaine across the living room one evening, 'this is the first time we've sat down as a family to watch a film together.'

'Is it?' Blaine replied with a warm smile spread across his face. The seemingly minor event felt worthy of note, and our first roast dinner at the table went by in the same fashion, with quiet recognition. The first time we took Jordan to play on the swings, I beamed with pride. It felt amazing to be just like any other family on a day out, but it was waving to him from the gates on his very first day of school that stuck out as a particularly special moment for me.

'Can you believe he's old enough to go to school?' I asked Blaine, stunned by how quick time seemed to be going. 'He'll be grown up before we know it.'

I may have missed the first steps he took and the first words he spoke, but every day I get to celebrate a new milestone with him. The first time he needed help with his homework, I was there to look over it, spending most nights sat down at the table with Jordan and his books. When it came time for getting his first pet, I was right by my little boy's side when, to mine and Blaine's amusement, he picked out a pet rat.

Every day I wake up feeling lucky, free from the past, excited to spend the day with the people I love most. The rest of my life will be full of seeing Jordan experience the world around him and I cannot wait to be there for him throughout it all.

Through my little boy I am witnessing a childhood I never had. My innocence was stolen from me at such a young age that I had almost forgotten what a normal upbringing looked like, but seeing Jordan play games and watch cartoons without a care in the world brings tears to my eyes. All I care about now is making sure he gets his childhood. I don't need anything else to make me happy, I finally have my dream family.

# 20.

# BUILDING A FUTURE

**O**f course, moving on is never as straightforward as it might seem. I would love nothing more than to forget the past but the damage the abuse has done to me is something that won't ever go away. It permeates everything I do, whether I like it or not. Both my time with Amanda and the years spent at New Hall taught me to toughen myself up and bury any vulnerability deep inside, and that is something I'm still trying to unlearn. I battle daily to try to be more open about my feelings but even something as simple as showing my family affection is a conscious act I often have to remind myself to do. Any slight gesture of human contact can be a huge trigger for me and no one in my life truly understands just how difficult that makes it for me to connect with my son.

I love Jordan more than anything else in the world, but

sometimes it's like my brain won't let me express it. There are times when I can be sat on the sofa with my family and all I want to do is cuddle up with Blaine and Jordan, but I can't move. It's as if I become paralysed, trapped in my own body, like I'm broken and I don't know how to fix it. *Does Amanda know what she's done to me? Do the men realise how much they have affected me? Do they know how hard it is to cuddle my son?*

Over a decade after I first saw Amanda smoking at the market stalls, I'm still living with the trauma she has left me with and I want everyone to know what she has put me through. Amanda may have got twelve years inside for what she did but she took far more than that away from me. I'm still living through the aftermath of her abuse, and the effects of what she did ripple through my life every day.

In particular, I am most distrusting of anyone around Jordan, constantly convincing myself that something bad will happen and I won't be there to stop it. Sometimes, if I take Jordan to the park, I'll even catch myself glaring at other adults. I look around at everyone in the area before spotting someone near the playground who doesn't have a child with them. Immediately my mind races. Why the fuck are you here? I rage to myself, my blood boiling. I gear myself up to confront them but then, before I move, I see a kid run over into the stranger's arms and I have to force myself to take a step back, trying to calm down. What is wrong with me? I wonder, unable to relax. It's almost impossible to enjoy a day out without looking over my shoulder, suspicious of anyone who so much as glances in our direction.

Jordan is now five years old, the same age I was when I was first sexually abused by Emily, and that notion petrifies me. I look at his tiny, innocent, beautiful face and I pray nothing will ever happen to him. The constant fear I have of anyone hurting him is exhausting, and I often worry to the point where it makes me sick. I'm even terrified of getting into taxis; the thought of being out of control and putting my safety into the hands of a stranger is almost too much to bear.

So many of the men involved in the sex ring weren't convicted, and every time I leave the house I check over my shoulder to make sure no one is following me. What if I see someone I recognise? I worry to myself. What if they find out I have a son? I'm terrified of taking Jordan to Sheffield to visit my family for that very reason, panic-stricken at the thought of seeing someone I used to know. *What if they recognise me but I don't remember them? What if they find out which school Jordan goes to?* My mind races with 'what ifs' constantly and it's an inner torment I struggle with daily. I wish I could stop myself but I can't help it – this is the reality of what my abusers have done. I suffer it every single day and for the time being at least I'm finding it very difficult to change my way of thinking.

I had been so conditioned to believe I deserved what happened to me that even now, all these years later, I'm still working through the truth. For a long time I would self-harm as a way to punish myself for how my life had turned out. It wasn't until years after Amanda's sentencing that I watched a film about child grooming, when the reality of what happened to me really sank in. I was a child when Emily assaulted me, and I was still a child when Amanda groomed me. None of this was my fault. A lot of my older tattoos are other forms of self-harm but the newer ones are covering up scars. It's taking a long time but I'm slowly realising that I don't need to be punished. I'm a victim, and even just being able to recognise that fact is how I know I'm healing. Getting over the abuse will be a lifelong battle, I know that, but I'm ready to fight. I deal with my anxiety by making sure Jordan is as aware of the dangers in the world as he can be.

'Remember that Mum and Dad must always know secrets, even if somebody says you can't tell us,' I remind him frequently. 'We will always believe you.' I'm carefully carving a close relationship with Jordan, mindful that if he ever needs someone to confide in, I'll always be there to listen. I sometimes reflect that if I had had someone to depend on when I was younger, things might not have turned out the way they did. I often wonder if there were signs I was being abused. Or did I manage to hide it? There's no way to truly know, but surely there were grown-ups around me who might have suspected. Growing up in care, however, I slipped through the system.

I had been so young and impressionable, with no one else to guide me, and Amanda became the person I thought

I could count on. Little did I know that she relied on my naivety, using her flash lifestyle to lure me into her clutches, but how could I have known any better? I was just a kid, and the immature idea I had in my head of wealth and happiness just wasn't realistic. Now I don't need money or material things because I get to wake up to Jordan and Blaine every day. We don't have much but this life is ours and we've built it together. On my down days, when I start to feel low, all I have to do is go into the living room at teatime. Blaine and Jordan are usually running around, play-fighting or acting silly together, and the whole house is filled with squeals of noise and laughter. I spend my days chasing Jordan around the house, trying to get him to stay still long enough so I can brush his teeth or run him a bath. The house is full to the brim with Jordan's toys; he's outgrowing them faster than I can tidy them up. But at the end of the day, when I sit down on the sofa, sandwiched between Blaine and Jordan as we watch a film together, I am complete. This is my family and, despite everything that has happened in the past, they love me unconditionally.

The way I envision my recovery is as a long, straight road that I'm walking along. Every now and then I stop and turn around, staring at the street behind me. I can just about see the past, lurking like a dot in the distance, but it never completely disappears. If I squint my eyes, focusing on the background, I can just about see the evil men, the drugs, the petrifying houses, and I pause for just a second to take it all in. But then I turn away and keep walking. Every time I look back again, it becomes harder to see. I'm not quite where I want to be but I'm still moving, and there's so much ground yet to cover. There's so much I still want to do with my life, my dream job being to work with elderly and disabled people. I'd like to be someone who can make sure vulnerable people are cared for and one day I'll get there.

Every day I take another step forward towards the future I'm creating and that, for me, is success. It may have taken a while but I'm slowly rebuilding my life, and I'm now pregnant again with another little boy. We're naming him Quinlan and I'm already so in love with him. I can't wait to welcome our little boy into our family. Jordan is due to become a big brother and he is beside himself with excitement. Watching him chat away to my stomach or ask me questions about the baby fills my heart with joy. As my bump grows, so does our family, and I'm so excited for our new addition. I hope the baby will bring Jordan and me even closer together, bonding over the new arrival. Finding out our baby was a boy, a huge sigh of relief washed over me. Of course, I'd love to have a little girl one day but, after everything I've been through, the thought alone is also my biggest fear. Nonetheless, I'm over the moon and, even though I've done this all before with Jordan, it feels different this time. When Quinlan is born, social services won't be waiting to take him away; the only people there will be his family. I won't be forced to say my goodbyes on the maternity ward. Instead I'll be taking my baby home with me, to his dad and brother, just where he belongs.

# BUILDING A FUTURE

I have an image in my head of what the future could look like – Blaine and me living in a house with a big garden, the kids growing up playing football on the grass, Jordan and Quinlan being the best of friends. For the first time it feels like my dreams could become reality. I can't reach them yet but I can just about touch them, and there's nothing on earth that could make me let go.

When I look back at the years spent with Amanda, in a way I consider myself lucky. I got out. There were other girls trapped in the sex ring who didn't have the same outcome. Girls who had been badly beaten and left for dead; girls who never saw their attacker stand trial. I escaped the clutches of the Sheffield sex ring and my main abuser is behind bars. I confided in someone at HMP New Hall and I was believed.

Around the time I reported Amanda, Operation Alphabet had already been set up by police. It was a special investigation into child sexual exploitation in South Yorkshire and one of the police officers involved, Paul Badger, was with me every step of the way. I wasn't the only one who got justice; Amanda was also convicted for the sexual exploitation of four other girls, the youngest being just eleven at the time. We were able to take down our abuser but there are still so many young and vulnerable girls being raped and violated across Britain every day. I want to make sure no girl ever has to go through the abuse I suffered at the hands of Amanda, and the only way to start is for me to speak out. Back then I didn't have a voice, but I won't be silenced any longer. For far too long, girls like me have been expected to remain quiet, almost accepting the mistreatment we received, but I refuse to live in my abuser's shadow forever.

I'm finally ready to close the chapter on Amanda. At the end of the day, I'm busy rushing around, tidying up the house before taking Jordan to bed. I give him a cuddle, tucking him into his superhero duvet before planting a goodnight kiss on his forehead. Once he's settled I head back downstairs and, finally in a moment of calm, I put my feet up. Blaine sits beside me and rests his hand on my heavily pregnant belly and, suddenly, I feel a kick. It's like electricity, a spark of something entirely new. That tiny kick is a brief glimpse at a brand new life that hasn't even started yet, not just for Quinlan but for me too, for all of us. I'm leaving the life of abuse behind me now because I have a new one to begin.

# EPILOGUE

When it was first suggested to me that I should write a book about my ordeal, I didn't know what to think. Throughout my darkest times, hearing other people's experiences was a great comfort and I have always found therapy in reading books similar to mine. They helped me realise that I wasn't alone, but I never even considered I would be able to write a book myself.

To me, my experiences were nothing out of the ordinary. Growing up conditioned to believe I deserved the horrors that happened to me, I didn't think anyone would care about my story. How wrong I was.

I'll never understand why it happened to me, whether I was just in the wrong place at the wrong time, or if I was just another vulnerable girl who slipped through the system. For years I blamed myself, but I know now it was never my fault. I was just a child looking for a friend.

# PIMPED

I know at times my story has been uncomfortable to read but these horrors of child abuse are real and still happening, so I thank you for doing so. There are many people who wanted to silence me, wanted me to keep quiet about the things I suffered, but you have lent your ear and listened to me when so many others refused. For that, I am so grateful.

Since writing my story, my life has changed all over again. I gave birth to our second child, Quinlan. He came into our lives on 28 September at 5.23 a.m. and at 5 lb 8 oz, our tiny baby was perfect. Blaine and I are so in love with our baby boy and Jordan is thrilled to be a big brother. Watching my sons bond with each other is both surreal and wonderful. My daily life is now a mountain of nappies and bath times and love – and I wouldn't change it for the world.

I will always be a survivor but now, even more importantly, I'm a mother. Waking up every morning to the sound of a chattering six-year-old and the nonsensical gurgling of a baby is like music to my ears. My boys have given me purpose, and that makes everything that has led to this point worthwhile.

My story is still far from finished. There's so much more to come but, for now, I'm content to sit back and take it all in. Harbouring the past is like carrying around a constant reminder of bad times, but now it's time for me to create happy memories. The wonder of normal life hasn't worn off on me yet and I intend for things to stay that way.

# ACKNOWLEDGEMENTS

I'd like to thank everyone who had a hand in making this book happen: Rikki Loftus, for helping me to put my story on paper; Kerri Sharp, my editor at John Blake; Clare Hulton, my literary agent; and Jack Falber at Medavia, for getting in touch and suggesting that I share my story with the world. I'm also grateful to Helen O'Brien, for taking the time to read through the drafts of my manuscript.

On a personal note, I'd like to thank Paul Badger, the police officer who was with me throughout my journey to justice. Paul was one of the first people to believe my story and, without him, I wouldn't be where I am today. I'd also like to thank my sister, Toni, and my best friend, Chantelle, who have both always been there for me.

However, the biggest thank you of all must go to my partner, Blaine Hibbert. It has been a rollercoaster but Blaine has stood by my side no matter what. He has never given up on me and I love him with all my heart.